DECISIONSCAPE

DECISIONSCAPE

How Thinking Like an Artist Can Improve Our Decision-Making

ELSPETH KIRKMAN

The MIT Press
Cambridge, Massachusetts
London, England

The MIT Press would like to thank the anonymous peer reviewers who provided comments on drafts of this book. The generous work of academic experts is essential for establishing the authority and quality of our publications. We acknowledge with gratitude the contributions of these otherwise uncredited readers.

To protect the anonymity of those who have participated in the author's research, many of the names have been changed in the descriptions of fieldwork.

This book was set in Adobe Garamond Pro by New Best-set Typesetters Ltd. Printed and bound in the United States of America.

Library of Congress Cataloging-in-Publication Data

Names: Kirkman, Elspeth, author.
Title: Decisionscape : how thinking like an artist can improve our decision-making / Elspeth Kirkman.
Description: Cambridge, Massachusetts : The MIT Press, [2024] | Includes bibliographical references and index.
Identifiers: LCCN 2023028465 (print) | LCCN 2023028466 (ebook) | ISBN 9780262048941 (hardcover) | ISBN 9780262378253 (epub) | ISBN 9780262378246 (pdf)
Subjects: LCSH: Decision making.
Classification: LCC BF448 .K53 2024 (print) | LCC BF448 (ebook) | DDC 153.8/3—dc23/eng/20230731
LC record available at https://lccn.loc.gov/2023028465
LC ebook record available at https://lccn.loc.gov/2023028466

10 9 8 7 6 5 4 3 2 1

For Imogen and Evie

Contents

INTRODUCTION: A SENSE OF PERSPECTIVE

1 THE ROAD TO BRUNELLESCHI

Forty-five and a half thousand years ago, the Upper Paleolithic was in full swing. The continent that would become North America was blanketed by glaciers. And half a million years after first emerging, *Homo sapiens* was finally making real progress in its global expansion out of Africa. As part of this great migration, a band of modern humans had settled around the equator on what is now the Indonesian island of Sulawesi. There was nothing about this particular group—ancestral vessels of our DNA, whose daily existence would have been unimaginably bleak—that suggested they would leave a mark on history. But, through some fluke of preservation and discovery, they left us one of the most important artifacts of prehistory: the earliest known example of figurative art.[1]

The figure in question is an animal. It looks, as rendered by its primitive artist, like a cross between a hedgehog and a coconut, although experts identify it as a "warty pig," a species native to Sulawesi and its surrounding islands. The pig, and other similar paintings in the region, transformed our understanding of human evolution: it tells us that we had the ability and motivation to document the world around us even before *Homo sapiens* dominated our Neanderthal cousins out of existence.

Flash forward 30,000 years to the southwest of modern-day France, and we were still painting animals on cave walls, only with much more elaborate results. The caves in Lascaux, discovered in September 1940, contain almost 2,000 figures, including a bull that is over sixteen feet long. It isn't just the volume and size of the paintings that is remarkable. Despite the crudeness of the tools and medium, they show how much more sophisticated our representations of the world had become. Most notably, the artists in Lascaux had begun experimenting with something we take for granted today: perspective.

Their attempts were simplistic but effective. Many of the animals overlap one another, creating a basic sense of depth. The size of individual animals in groups also suggests that they were experimenting with scaling objects to show distance from the viewer. For instance, some herd animals are smaller and painted in less vivid detail than those in the foreground (figure 1.1).

Overlapping cattle was just the start. As artists and their work came out of caves and into the foundations of modern society, it became clear that this drive to capture a likeness of the world around us was a foundational part of human nature. And yet, despite huge innovations in style and materials, we were stymied in one important way: the things we drew just didn't look *real*. To create a convincing illusion of real space, we needed to figure out how to recreate depth on a flat page. This quest would take us on a journey spanning millennia and drawing in geometricians, and artists, architects, and philosophers.

Figure 1.1
Photograph of cave wall at Lascaux, France: Aurochs, horses, and deer, Wikimedia Commons License (https://commons.wikimedia.org/wiki/File:Lascaux_painting.jpg).

Over the years the various pieces of the puzzle were discovered and lost again, until eventually the stochastic forces of fate created the conditions for it all to come together. This chapter tells the story of how this happened.

It is worth beginning by being clear that we see depth in the real world naturally. This happens through a process called *binocular vision*. By combining information from both eyes, we build an accurate picture of depth and distance by cross-referencing the parts where the inputs overlap. We learn to do this very early in life. Babies can detect patterns of lights that can only be seen using binocular vision by the time they are about four months old,[2] even if they were born prematurely: the binocular module comes preinstalled—we just need to get enough experience with depth cues to fire it up.

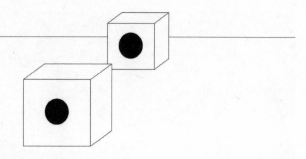

Figure 1.2
Cube and dot illusion.

But our ability to interpret representations of depth is harder to acquire. In part, this may be because the things depicted in *pictorial space* are not always familiar to young children. For example, when shown an image like the one in figure 1.2, adults tend to report that the central dot on the smaller cube is larger than the central dot on the larger cube. Children, though, are more likely to correctly report that the dots are the same size.[3]

When we believe, as adults do, that the smaller cube is farther away in space, we also believe the dot on its surface to be distant. Since the dots are the same size on the page, our brain automatically assumes the "background" dot is larger. A child may not yet assume this relationship between the dots and the cubes, or even the lines themselves, meaning they see the objects in the picture more independently than an adult who understands the conventions of drawing.

Trickery aside, the cube diagram shows just how little it takes to induce the illusion of three dimensions on a two-dimensional page. Consider another simple image, this time of a railway track (figure 1.3). This image creates the illusion of

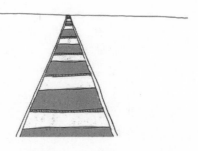

Figure 1.3
Railway track sketch using one-point linear perspective.

three dimensions using the simplest form of *perspective projection*: *one-point linear perspective*. It is the kind of image that a child could recreate in minutes. It is also the kind of image our ancestors failed to produce over tens of thousands of years with a paintbrush. This picture uses a few simple geometric tricks to produce its effect. First, and most obviously, the objects in the picture, such as the sleepers on the track, get smaller with distance. This effect is known as *diminution*, and it is what the artists in the caves of Lascaux were trying out all those millennia ago when they made the animals in the back of the herd appear smaller. Effective diminution cannot be achieved through intuition alone. It requires geometric precision. To establish the horizontal space an object should occupy as it becomes more distant, the artist needs to identify a single *vanishing point*: a spot on the horizon at which the parallel lines of the drawing converge. In this image, the train tracks show how this works: in real space, we know the tracks run parallel to one another, remaining an equal distance apart, but in the pictorial space I can easily create the illusion of depth and distance by bringing them together as they recede toward the horizon. These

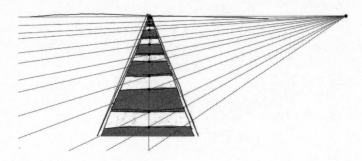

Figure 1.4
Railway track with transversal lines overlaid.

converging parallel track lines define the bounds within which
the sleepers should lie.

To achieve accurate diminution, an artist also needs to
know how much vertical space on the page their objects should
occupy. This requires the use of a different set of parallel lines,
this time radiating out from the picture's *distance points*. Figure
1.4 shows how this works.

As well as helping determine the vertical dimensions of
diminution, the relationship between the vanishing point and
the distance points also tells the artist about the optimal *viewpoint*: the place at which a viewer should stand to enjoy the
illusion to maximum effect. Together, these simple geometric
techniques allow the artist to produce convincing diminution,
leading us as viewers to see the tracks in three dimensions.

The resulting illusion is powerful. To show how powerful,
we can add two extra horizontal lines (figure 1.5). This is known
as the *Ponzo illusion*.[4] Just as the dots in figure 1.2 were the same
size, the lines are the same length; measure them with a ruler if
you don't believe me. But because our brains automatically see the
image in three dimensions, we perceive the top line to be longer.

Figure 1.5
Railway track with the Ponzo illusion overlaid.

Not everyone, however, falls for the illusion. When shown an image, like the one above, students from Pennsylvania State University were almost twice as likely as students at the University of Guam to report that the lines were different lengths.[5] When this research was conducted in the 1960s, the perceptual difference was attributed to the fact that most of the Guamanian students would not have seen railroad tracks in real life. While interesting, this theory is weak: the Guamanian students would certainly have had enough familiarity with roads, buildings, and other rectilinear shapes to be able to handle the concept of a railroad. What they may have had less familiarity with, though, is the conventions of pictorial space. Chamorro art—that is, the art of the Indigenous Guamanians—is notably lacking in geometric depth construction. They may simply have not known how to "read" two-dimensional representations of depth.

Fortunately, the researchers were also skeptical of their hypothesis, and in 1972 they reran the study, this time in Uganda.[6] Their two populations were Ugandan students at the university of Makerere and people who lived in villages surrounding the capital of Kampala. Both the villagers and the university students lived and worked in "carpentered" environments chock-full of depth cues. But most of the villagers had little to no exposure to two-dimensional representations of depth. As expected, the villagers were duped far less frequently by the Ponzo illusion than their educated compatriots. Fluency with *representations* of depth, it seems, was the driving force behind the cognitive error.

Beyond familiarity with the conventions of perspective projection, other aspects of culture also appear to make us more or less susceptible to these illusions. For example, in a 2019 study, French participants were more often tricked by an illusion where a corridor receded into the distance from left to right, while Syrian participants were more easily duped by a corridor receding right to left.[7] This phenomenon is attributed to the way each group has learned to scan the page when reading or writing: left to right in French, and right to left in Arabic.

The insight that interpreting depth on a page is a learned skill may go some of the way toward explaining why it took so long for humans to figure out how to represent three dimensions in two: if we wouldn't instantly be sure when we saw it, how could we work toward creating a convincing illusion? But while it is certainly the case that the underpinning geometric principles cannot be easily intuited based on our experience of natural vision, it isn't that no one could decode them. Around 300 BC, the Greek mathematician Euclid wrote a work called *Optics* that described almost everything an artist would need to create perspective projection in their work. But his insights didn't seem to make it into the proto-art studios of ancient Greece.

This failure to transmit may have been down to a second factor that explains why it took such a long time to master the illusion of depth: artists just didn't care that much about realism in their work. For much of our history with a paintbrush, art was not focused on recreating an accurate likeness of the world around us. Instead, although its function varied across time and cultures, art was generally used for documentary or religious purposes. That is, art typically either captured the basic activities of everyday life or glorified religious figures and events. Since no value was placed on realism, developing ways to create rational space on the page was not prioritized or rewarded. Perspective projection, it turns out, is not as neutral as it seems. Its emergence and use tell us about the values of the artist and their world.

So, we can see that art was not lacking per se; it just used systems and conventions that didn't prize realism. In ancient Egypt, for example, artists presented all figures on a single plane, using the relative size of the figures to convey their importance. In this way, the largest figures—often gods—were the obvious subject of the picture, while smaller figures and details, such as slaves or possessions, were to be interpreted as accompanying detail. Since the style did not demand background details or consideration of the space the figures occupied, there was limited need for the artist to worry about creating a sense of pictorial depth (figure 1.6).

As time passed, the idea of presenting a whole scene in which figures occupied a specific space became more important. The Romans figured out receding parallel lines, although the vanishing point appears to have escaped them. The geometric insights needed to produce convincing pictorial space were

Figure 1.6
Procession of figures with offerings. Part of a wall painting from the tenth tomb at Gourna, Thebes (Pharaonic era). Sketch made during an expedition to Egypt organized by Robert Hay between 1826 and 1838, Wikimedia Commons License (https://upload.wikimedia.org/wikipedia/commons/4/43/Egyptian_tomb_wall-painting_-_Egyptian_Collections%2C_Vol._XI_%281826-1838%29%2C_f.118_-_BL_Add_MS_29822.jpg).

also refined. In the eleventh century, more than a thousand years after Euclid, the Islamic mathematician, Ibn al-Haytham wrote his *Book of Optics*, codifying everything an artist needed to know to produce the illusion of three-dimensional space. But, despite this geometric innovation, the Middle Ages rumbled on and art—whose purpose was now largely religious—remained stubbornly flat. And so it was that millennia after those prehistoric hands drew overlapping cattle, we still found ourselves unable to effectively represent depth in two dimensions (figure 1.7).

Then, in fifteenth-century Florence, almost 40,000 years after the warty pig in Sulawesi, along came Filippo Brunelleschi. Brunelleschi was an architect, and he wanted to be able to easily compare his attempts to draw buildings with the real deal. His solution was ingeniously simple: cut a hole in a picture of a building and look through to see the reflection of the

Figure 1.7
Duccio di Buoninsegna, *Last Supper* (1308–1311), Wikimedia Commons
License (https://commons.wikimedia.org/wiki/File:Duccio_di_Buoninsegna_-_
Last_Supper_-_WGA06786.jpg).

image in a hand mirror, behind which was the building itself.
By adjusting the distance between the mirror and the drawing,
Brunelleschi could get it to look the same size in the mirror as
the real structure behind. This way he could move his hand
with the mirror out of the way and play an elaborate game of
"spot the difference" with the marble-clad original.

Brunelleschi's approach uncovered the elusive vanishing
point: that single place to which all the parallel lines of the drawing recede. The insight was as radical as it was simple, immediately and dramatically improving the quality of the pictures.

Brunelleschi's training and inventiveness gave him the means to crack the code of perspective, but it was the conditions of the early 1400s that gave him the opportunity and the motive. Rationalism was king, and with it came a desire to represent the world with a greater degree of fidelity in art. The subjects of art were also diversifying. While religion was still a huge feature in most Europeans' lives and continued to dominate art, secular life was becoming richer and more culturally significant. Suddenly, it was important to be able to accurately capture cityscapes, social interactions, and commercial scenes. This shift in interests and values was paralleled by a kind of existential obsession with understanding space and distance. Until this point, for most people, the world had been local and predictable—a few fields or streets, the turn of the seasons, a small tribe of familiar faces—and we had been the center of the map. Now, at the dawn of the Age of Discovery, the perimeters of that map were expanding as fast as we could document them and we found ourselves, in the truest sense, *dislocated*, the vast distances we now had to comprehend stretching our sense of space beyond its elastic limit. This shake-up was not confined to the geographic horizon. Society itself was being radically rearranged. The Black Death had killed a third of the European continent and catalyzed the decline of serfdom, creating a new middle class and centralizing power in a way that allowed Western Europe's monarchies to amass enormous wealth. Navigating these societal shocks of the Renaissance required a kind of agility of perspective, and the appeal of being able to create and control our representation of space, distance, and depth must have been powerful.

Brunelleschi's approach was embraced fairly immediately by his contemporaries in Florence, but without codifying the precise method for achieving linear perspective, its ability to spread further was curtailed. It was not Brunelleschi who undertook the work of mathematical documentation for his method but his friend and fellow architect, Leon Battista Alberti. Alberti dedicated his treatise, *On Painting*, to Brunelleschi. In it he introduced the theory behind linear perspective in enough practical detail for any artist who laid their hands on it to recreate the effect. The work was a slow burn, encountering two major barriers when it was first written. First, Alberti's decision to write in Latin meant that many Renaissance painters simply could not read the text. Second, he finished writing the treatise around fifteen years before the advent of the European printing press, which limited distribution. In time, though, the work was translated and mass-produced. Eventually, it made its way into the hands of the men who would come to define the High Renaissance: Michelangelo, Leonardo da Vinci, and Raphael. Their works changed art forever, and the journey to establish perspective projection techniques was complete.

2 THE DECISIONSCAPE

As someone who studies decision-making, I see a lot of parallels between the art world's frustrated quest for perspective projection and the predictable struggles we all have when it comes to forming our own perspectives. I am not alone in observing this similarity. Knowingly or not, we often draw on the logic of pictorial space as a metaphor for our decisions. We use phrases like *getting things in perspective* or *blowing them out of proportion*. We *center* or *foreground* specific features of a decision. And we implore one another to *zoom out* or *see the big picture*. The links between perspective projection and decision-making run deeper than these turns of phrase, though. When we make choices, we are like an artist rearranging objects on the canvas, using our own system of perspective to compose a mental representation of the world around us. This mental representation operates in much the same way as pictorial space. First, psychologically distant aspects of a decision are drawn smaller than those that are proximal. Second, we see things from a specific and fixed viewpoint. Third, the composition of the picture—that is, the way its details are arranged to make a coherent whole—influences the overall impression. And, finally, like the artist choosing their subject, we are influenced by wider forces in the world around us. I call this mental representation *the decisionscape*, and the central idea of this book is that we could improve our decisions, whether personal or professional, by constructing and analyzing it deliberately, just as an artist approaches the canvas.

If this idea of the decisionscape is a little abstract, ask yourself: What made you buy this book? Was it the cover? The price? The placement on the shelf? Maybe you thought it seemed the sort thing you *should* read? Or perhaps someone got it for you as a gift, thinking it might tell you something about how they see you. Whatever the reason, you have this book in your hand as the result of a range of different factors that won out in your decisionscape. To understand how these factors exert their influence, imagine each of the books you could have chosen drawn on a canvas. Making a choice involves assessing each book against several factors that determine where you should place it. Books that score well against the factors that are most important to you—your preferred genre or length, for example—end up drawn larger in the foreground. Books that score less well are shunted into the distance, diminished in size. All of this happens instantaneously without you expending very much effort at all.

Even at this simple level, it is easy to see that no two decisionscapes are the same. You might like detective novels, while I like cheesy romance. Just as the arrangement of the decisionscape differs from person to person, we also find that we are inconsistent in ourselves much of the time. If I am buying a book to read on the beach, for example, my requirements will be different than if I am choosing something to share with my highly intellectual book club. Books are a great example of how we make choices that reinforce our ideas of who we are and also play to how we want others to see us. I have dozens of worthy books that I have bought, read a brief extract from, and then left to gather dust over the years. And yet each time I go to a book shop, the abstract notion of myself as someone who reads heavyweight ideas seduces me to buy things I will never read beyond the preface.

The contents of the decisionscape are also bounded in ways we do not notice or control. For example, if the global publishing industry is only interested in releasing books about crime, celebrity, and history, then the shelves I browse will be tightly curated in a way that is invisible to me. This introduces another idea: the decisionscape can be applied to institutions as much as it can to individuals. After all, a publisher is made up of a collection of people who make decisions in the interest of the business and in the context of the wider industry. These commercial and cultural forces also send signals about what is "normal" and acceptable to read. I might, for example, really want to read only young adult fiction, but the covers clearly designed for teenagers make me feel too embarrassed to read it on the bus. In this case it would turn out that conformity is something I pay a lot of attention to in my decisionscape, making the YA books inch toward the background in shame.

This is not an exhaustive list of the factors that buffet and shape the options in your decisionscape. Thousands of tiny things shape our decisions throughout the course of each day. Most of them go completely unnoticed. We operate on a sophisticated autopilot that guides us through the world without expending unnecessary effort. But the downside is that we don't notice warping forces in our decisions. We make small and predictable mistakes in our judgment that cause some options to look larger or smaller than they really are. We are like the pre-Brunelleschian artist: almost getting the perspective right but not quite nailing it. For the remainder of this chapter, I will introduce the four main factors that shape our decisionscapes, the ways they can trip us up, and what we can do about it.

Up first, the subject of the first part of this book: distance and diminution.

Over the years, viewers of art have absorbed the unspoken logic of the canvas, understanding—for example—that we should pay most attention to the details of those things that are foregrounded or placed in such a way that draws the eye. In Leonardo da Vinci's *The Last Supper*, for example, Christ's face is centered at the vanishing point so that even someone unfamiliar with his cultural importance would know that he was the main character among the thirteen people at the table. Like the artist, we put those factors that loom largest in the foreground of our decisions, placing everything else relative to them. As things become more psychologically distant, on the other hand, they take up less mental space. Psychological distance can take many forms, of which spatial distance is just one. For example, *social distance* means I might foreground the consequences of a decision on a friend but minimize any effect I might have on a stranger. *Temporal distance* causes me to think about events in the future or past in a way that is different than present events, which loom large. And if I think something is unlikely to happen, I experience a sense of *hypothetical distance* compared to events that are very likely.

While this idea of psychological distances may seem unremarkable, the fact we are able to traverse them is anything but. The ability to transcend the confines of the time and space in which we live, to relate to others in a deep way, and to rehearse potential outcomes that may never come to be are all highly sophisticated and, at least collectively, almost certainly unique to humans. Our fluid ability to navigate these four types of distance—temporal, spatial, social, and hypothetical—enables us to conjure multidimensional representations of our world.

Interestingly, the rules underpinning how we perceive different types of psychological distance have clear parallels to the geometric principles that govern how we perceive spatial distance. Look, for example, at how our preferences shift as time passes. A classic intertemporal choice experiment, for example, might offer half its participants (group A) a choice between $30 in a week and $40 in eight days while offering the other half (group B) a choice between $30 this afternoon or $40 tomorrow afternoon.[1] In both cases, the real question is whether you think it is worth waiting twenty-four hours for an extra $10, but these experiments consistently show that participants in groups A and B behave differently. Group A is more patient, waiting eight days for the $40, while group B wants the more instant gratification of the $30 available in a few hours. On the face of it, this makes little sense, so why do the two options look different the closer we get? The answer suggests that the parallels between our experience of spatial and psychological distance are more than metaphorical. It turns out that visual perception distorts as we draw closer to an object in more or less the same way as temporal perception does in these intertemporal choice experiments. With thanks to my colleague Toby

Park for providing this analogy, consider two conifer trees in a forest. The first tree is 30 feet tall. A little way behind it is a second tree, standing 40 feet tall. If you walk toward both trees head-on, you will be able to tell that the farther one is taller, despite the dwarfing effect of distance. However, as you get closer to the first, shorter, conifer, something odd begins to happen. Each step opens up the angle at which you are viewing it, causing the tree to loom larger and larger in your vision. At some point, you perceive the top of the closer tree to be higher than that of the tree behind it. You still know, of course, that the second tree is bigger, just as you know that $40 is worth more than $30. It just doesn't *appear* that way in the moment the foreground takes over.

Part 2 of this book focuses on the role of viewpoint in our decisions. Just as the receding lines of pictorial space only create the illusion of depth when viewed from a specific angle, so each of us is the origin of the psychological distances represented in our decisionscapes. In other words, when we talk about psychological distance, we are describing something egocentric. This means that the placement of specific objects in our decisionscapes often says as much about the decision-maker as it does about the objective facts of the decision inputs. The presentation may seem neutral, but we are really like the artist moving their easel and adjusting the scene in front of them to find the right angle. As the old saying goes, "We see the world not as it is but as we are." Because of this, we often do our best thinking when we find ways to play with our perspective, shifting our viewpoint to see how things look from different angles.

Sometimes this happens naturally. For example, our viewpoint in any given moment is heavily influenced by our understanding of how we fit into wider society, an understanding that shapes what is known as our *social identity*. Each of us possesses many different social identities that we wear and take off throughout the day. In the morning, for example, my primary social identity is as a parent. During the day I am a worker. And in the evening, well, in the evening I am someone who watches too much TV. The social identity that is active in a given moment can change how we see the world around us. For example, everyone has a racial identity that may feel more or less salient at different times. This identity whirs in the background and changes how we perceive those around us. For example, we tend to recognize the faces of people who are the same race as us with more precision than those who are not. One might hypothesize that this is about familiarity; perhaps we have just had more exposure to people of our own race. Research, however, shows this is also likely due to an imbalance in how much attention we pay to the faces of those we perceive to be socially close to us versus those who are more socially distant. In the case of race, this means we mentally sort people into buckets of "like me" and "not like me." Individuals in the "like me" bucket are more psychologically proximal to us, and so we expend energy on learning their individually identifying details. The people in the "not like me" bucket are distant. They do not get this extra attention and remain a homogeneous group.

This has real implications for how we experience society. For example, we might overestimate the number of people in a marginalized community because we consider them to be a monolithic "other." Researchers Rebecca Ponce de Leon, Jacqueline Rifkin, and Richard Larrick use this insight to explain why people overestimate the number of Jews at the University of Pennsylvania; the lesbian population of an Atlanta suburb; and the number of Asians studying at Duke University.[2] This phenomenon of classifying people based on whether they are "similar" or "other" is so powerful that it can be induced using arbitrarily assigned identities. To explore this, Jay Van Bavel at New York University and William Cunningham at Ohio State University recruited a set of participants and told them that they were part of a group called "the Suns" before telling them about the existence of a rival group, "the Moons."[3] The members of the Suns were then assigned different social roles. Half were told they were soldiers and that their job was to remain loyal to the Suns and serve the needs of their group. The other half were assigned the role of spy, whose ultimate goal was to serve the needs of their group by infiltrating the Moons. After group members were assigned their identities, they were shown twelve faces one by one on a computer screen. Each face was labeled as being affiliated with either the Suns or the Moons; the faces appeared in a random order and then disappeared from the screen after four seconds. After seeing the faces, the participants were shown a second set of twenty-four faces, half of which had appeared in the first batch. All they had to do was say whether they recognized the face from the previous batch. The researchers predicted that, because of their objective to infiltrate the Moons, the spies would pay more attention to the faces of those in the Moons than the soldiers. This would mean they would perform better in the recognition exercise than the soldiers, who would be using the standard approach of paying more attention to those in their in-group. This prediction turned out to be correct. What is perhaps more surprising, though, is that the spies' ability to recognize their rivals did not come at the expense of recognizing their own group: both soldiers and spies from the Suns were equally good at recognizing other Suns. This suggests that, although we can effortfully pay more attention to those in out-groups, we automatically encode information about in-groups without needing specific instruction.

This egocentric tint also affects other forms of psychological distance. For example, it turns out we think things are physically closer than they really are when we consider them to be threatening. In another study involving Jay Van Bavel, led by Yi Jenny Xiao, several American undergraduates were asked to estimate the distance between New York and Los Angeles, New York and Vancouver, and New York and Mexico City.[4] Before estimating these distances, they were also asked a range of questions about how strongly they identified as an American and the extent to which they agreed with statements about Mexican immigration posing a symbolic threat to America. To give an example of one of the questions: "Immigration from Mexico is undermining American culture, do you agree?" The researchers then looked at the relationship between patriotism, sentiment toward Mexican immigration, and the estimated distances. Their hypothesis was that those who strongly identified with American culture and perceived Mexican immigration as a threat to it would estimate Mexico City to be closer than those who do not see Mexican immigration as a threat. Los Angeles and Vancouver were included to test the hypothesis that the misjudgment in distance was related to anxiety about Mexican immigration. Los Angeles, as a US city, they reasoned, should be judged as equally close for both groups. Distance estimates of Vancouver as a nonthreatening foreign city should also be unaffected. The hypothesis was proven in the results. Mexico City *seemed* about 1,000 miles closer to those who considered Mexican immigrants to be a threat compared to those who did not, (interestingly, almost everyone vastly overestimated how far away Mexico City was in reality!). For Los Angeles and Vancouver, though, the estimates did not differ.

This study hints at how emotions can distort our decisionscapes. In terms of hypothetical distance, for example, if two scenarios—A and B—had the same outcome, we should pay more attention to whichever is most likely to play out. If one scenario is emotionally charged, though, it can dominate our attention even if the other has a higher probability of happening. This phenomenon, whereby our attention is drawn to the things that seem most emotionally grabbing, is known to psychologists as *availability bias*.[5] At the beach, for example, many of us have found ourselves imagining how our dangling legs look to a shark on the bottom of the ocean, but we rarely worry about drowning, which is more than 3,000 times more likely to kill us than a shark attack.[6] The emotional arousal induced by the thought of a shark makes it loom larger than the idea of drowning because of the amount of detail it conjures. We can vividly and viscerally imagine the mechanics of a shark attack while drowning remains more abstract.

Research by Nira Liberman and Yaacov Trope shows this relationship between psychological distance and detail is bound up with the concept of "construal level."[7] When we think about something, such as an event, we might do so in a way that engages in a high or low level of construal. High-level construal allows us to think more abstractly. For example, if I am planning a party to take place in a year—in other words, a temporally distant event—I might think about things like the theme, time of day, or type of venue. Low-level construal is all about the details. Once that party is a few weeks away, you know I will be stressing out about the seating arrangements, whether there will be enough food, or what the playlist should be. Similarly, the fundamental attribution error—a social phenomenon whereby individuals explain their own behaviors in terms of the situation they are in but attribute the behaviors of others to their fundamental character or traits—can be explained by the interplay between social distance and construal level.[8] Specifically, the distance between oneself and others makes it harder to imagine the concrete details of what drove the behavior, making it easier to gloss over important contextual factors that would feel highly salient if they were happening to oneself. In both these cases—planning the party or determining why someone has reacted a certain way—it is as though our brains experience the same mechanical limitation as the artist drawing small, distant objects: the farther away something gets, the harder it is to render the details. As such, the distant features of decisions and paintings will both inevitably use cruder brushstrokes.

But it isn't just that it gets harder to render detail. As something gets more distant, our entire conceptual understanding of what we are looking at can also change. Imagine you are standing in a forest. If I ask you to describe what you see right in front of you, in all likelihood you will say, "A tree." You will be able to give a detailed account of its bark and tell me about the smells you are experiencing or the way the light falls. If I ask you where you are standing, on the other hand, your perspective will zoom out, elevating your construal level and causing you to tell me you are in a forest. This is what happens when you "switch" construal levels. In our day-to-day lives we perform a constant stream of conceptual toggling like this. Think, for instance, of the expression "the days are long, but the years are short." This sensation of two different speeds of time arises because days and years are construed at different levels. The days are concrete and tediously detailed, but the years are marked by the general sense of how life felt at that time and by a small number of temporal milestones that stand out in the memory. Similarly, "the grass is always greener on the other side" because you can't see the details; in front of your feet is a patch of mud, but out in the distance it's only rolling meadows.

This interplay between the parts and the whole relates to artistic composition, the subject of part 3 of this book. In the mind and on the canvas, the effect of the individual details is different than the effect of how those details work together to form the whole picture. Consider the Street Gestalt Completion Task used by psychologists.[9] In psychology, *gestalt* is the word of choice to describe a situation (often an image) in which the whole is more than the sum of its parts. Figure 2.1 shows an example of how the Gestalt Completion Task works. When you take in the big picture, your brain tries to make sense of the black shapes collectively, revealing a puppy. If you look at the detail of each shape individually, though, you will find it much harder to work out what you were looking at. In other words, the detail adds up to a larger pattern, meaning you cannot succeed in the task unless you are engaged in a high level of construal.

Studies that use the Gestalt Completion Task can give an insight into how psychological distance can be invoked or

Figure 2.1

An example of an image used in the Street Gestalt Completion Task. Adapted from a figure in C. Piccini, R. Lauro-Grotto, M. M. Del Viva, and D. Burr, "Agnosia for Global Patterns: When the Cross-Talk Between Grouping and Visual Selective Attention Fails," *Cognitive Neuropsychology* 20, no. 1 (2003): 12.

collapsed to help us dial the level of abstraction up or down. In one study, for example, half the participants were told to spend five minutes imagining their lives a year from now before completing ten Gestalt Completion tasks.[10] The other half also completed the tasks but first spent time imagining their life tomorrow. In line with the researchers' hypothesis, the participants who focused on the immediate future were less able to solve the puzzles than those who thought about themselves a year from the test day. In other words, temporal distance from the assessment seemed to have a bearing on whether participants were able to see the big picture—the gestalt. The results of this study, and others, suggest something important: when we need to be strategic, take a long view, or be dispassionate, we will be much better equipped to do so if we are psychologically distant from factors that may have a bearing on our judgment. Imagine, for example, you are responsible for setting a ten-year vision for your company. Being in the weeds of the current organizational issues and politics is unlikely to help elevate your mindset to the level needed. On the other hand, if you were then tasked with figuring out a plan for implementing that strategy, you would be unable to succeed if you remained distant from the detail of the current context. All too often, in real-world decisions, we find ourselves at the wrong end of the construal telescope: either the consequences of a decision are too abstract, causing us to neglect and discount important factors, or we get too hung up on the details to zoom out effectively.

So far, I have explored parallels between the construction of pictorial space and our decisionscapes by looking at diminution, viewpoint, and composition. Each of these factors is, at least to some extent, within our control to shape. But our decisionscapes are also colored and framed by the wider social and cultural contexts within which we live. This idea of *the frame* is the subject of part 4 of this book. It explores the influential forces at work on our decisionscapes that go unnoticed. In art, for example, the stylistic choices made by the artist are often Trojan horses for the cultural values of the world they are depicting. In the last chapter, for example, I wrote about the ubiquitous adoption of Brunelleschian perspective in the West. But I left out a critical piece of the story: when Brunelleschi's technique made it to China, it was roundly rejected. Just as linear perspective emerged as an artistic response to the cultural demands of the European Renaissance, other systems rose as artifacts of their own cultural milieu. In China, a system called *parallel projection* was developed.

As figure 2.2 demonstrates, parallel projection does not show depth in a way that mimics human vision. For a start, as you can see from the roofs running from the bottom to the top of the frame, it does not require that objects diminish in size as they stretch into the distance, making it difficult to gauge depth

Figure 2.2

Xu Yang, *Marriage* (eighteenth century), Suzhou, China. An example of parallel projection, Wikimedia Commons License (https://commons.wikimedia.org /wiki/File:Xu_Yang_-_Marriage.jpg).

for the uninitiated. Second, parallel projection allows the artist to capture more than a single viewer would be capable of seeing. In this picture, for example, some of the background activity, such as the people in the square behind the foremost horizontal roof, would likely be blotted out by the foreground if realistic proportions were maintained. In other words, parallel projection eschews the fixed viewpoint that defines linear perspective. Chinese artist and teacher Kwo Da-Wei describes this stylistic choice as follows: "The Chinese concept of perspective, unlike the scientific view of the West, is an idealistic or suprarealistic approach, so that one can depict more than can be seen with the naked eye."[11] This is unsurprising in some ways. After all, one of the largest cultural differences between classic Eastern and Western philosophies is how Eastern philosophies value the ability to transcend the individual self. In Eastern religions, secular teachings, and societies, the ability to see yourself as part of a larger whole is celebrated and rewarded. When we consider this, the attention to realism in Western art seems less ideologically neutral than it might otherwise. By going to great pains to perfectly render a scene for a single viewer, Western artists reveal a reverence for the individual perspective. The parallel projection of Eastern art, by contrast, facilitates transcendence by offering a perspective wider than the tether of an individual viewpoint. Its refusal to represent distance as we see it echoes the drive for oneness that characterizes much of Eastern thought. In this tradition, the purpose of perspective in art is not to faithfully document the everyday but to elevate the viewer, allowing them to see the world in a more open way.

This may seem like an inconsequential and isolated example of how perspective can operate as a tool for communicating

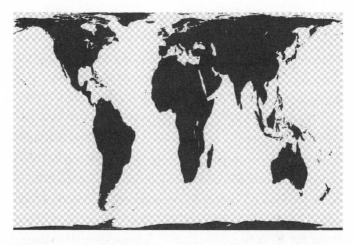

Figure 2.3
Gall-Peters projection world map. Wikimedia Commons License (https://commons.wikimedia.org/wiki/File:Peters_projection,_warm_grey.png).

social and cultural values. Consider, though, that much of the way we depict and understand the world is also bound up in choices we have made about what to emphasize and how to communicate the size of different aspects of a picture. The map in figure 2.3 gives a neat example.

To most of us, it looks like a distorted version of the Mercator projection—the world map we are used to seeing. North America looks withered while Africa and South America seem to have been overextended. The domineering Eurasian landmass is still impressive but rather less so than we have been led to expect. But this map—known as the Gall-Peters projection—is more accurate than the Mercator projection. Of course, it isn't perfect. Like any effort to represent the world on a flat page, it has had to make compromises. But it does give a much better sense of the relative size of the various landmasses we have carved up into countries and geopolitical regions. The Gall-Peters projection reminds us that the maps we use—their orientation, the countries they center, and which parts of the globe they draw in most detail—do more than simply reflect our understanding of the world. They reinforce it.

Maps also reinforce the point that artists—be they cartographers or those painting a royal portrait—don't randomly choose their subject matter or how to depict it. Every aspect of the work, from the materials to the perspective system chosen to the focal subjects to the arrangement of objects, reflects something about the world within which the art is being created. Our decisions are like this too. We don't start with a blank canvas. Instead, we consciously and nonconsciously factor in all kinds of external influences. Such forces alter what is foregrounded and focal, pushing other aspects of the decision into the distance or periphery. This language is deliberately literal. Our social preconceptions can literally alter how we see the things right before our eyes. In one study from the University of Lincoln (UK), for example, Caucasian women were asked to estimate the dress size of a range of female avatars.[12] The avatars, shown in a random order, were—in the language of the researchers—either Caucasian, Asian, or African. For each of the three races there was one avatar in every common dress size. All the women had to do was guess the dress size of each avatar. The results showed that African and Asian avatars were perceived to be larger than their identically sized Caucasian counterparts. For the smallest dress size (a UK size 6, US size 2), participants estimated African avatars to be almost a full dress size larger on average. This finding matched with the researchers' expectations. Their hypothesis was that the prevalence of thinness and white bodies in the cultural construction of beauty standards leads us to see bodies that are not white as larger because we perceive them to be farther away from that beauty standard. A similar phenomenon is seen when people are asked to estimate the size of their own bodies. In a study with adolescents, healthy young people tended to overestimate their body size by about 12 percent.[13] Adolescents with an eating disorder, however, thought they were about 30 percent larger than they really were. Both results suggest that our perception can be distorted by societal expectations and that this warping of perception is more extreme for those with disordered eating.

So far, I have largely talked about the decisionscape as though each of us is an artist, deliberately composing a piece of work. But the reality is that we are often more like the viewer, looking on as things pop up in the foreground without our having invited them. This is because our emotional and intuitive responses are fast, automatic, and often impossible to override. They sneak in well before our brains can fire up the conscious decision processes, displacing everything we might want to focus on in favor of what makes our palms sweat and our heart race. Just as someone looking at an optical illusion may rationally know that the lines are the same length, we cannot "unsee" our own perspectives, even when we know they are distorted. This all means that the mechanics of our judgment and decision-making can be as invisible to us as the need for a vanishing point was to the Roman artists. Just as we don't need to understand the geometry of perspective projection to interpret an artist's use of it, we don't need to understand how our decisionscapes are generated to navigate them. This automaticity serves us well most of the time. After all, we don't have enough mental energy to deliberate over every aspect of our decision-making. But when—like an artist making a painting—we need to be deliberate in our decisions, our inability to decode the mechanics of the decisionscape can also trip us up, causing us to misinterpret key inputs into our decisions.

In these cases, it is not enough to know that we are fallible or susceptible to predictable distortions. We need to design the external structures that support decision-making in ways that minimize the risk of undesirable error. Much has been written about this in the behavioral science literature. Most notably, in *Nudge* Richard Thaler and Cass Sunstein introduce the idea of "choice architecture," the notion that specific moments of choice are structured in ways that are never neutral and, moreover, that we can modify those structures for good.[14] To give a simple example, since changing the default so that workers now have to opt out of workplace retirement plans, millions of people in the United Kingdom are now saving for retirement who did not when they had to actively opt in.

More recently, Ruth Schmidt has challenged the field to expand the focus to "choice infrastructure," a systemic look at how the wider ecosystem within which we make a whole range of choices influences our decisions and what we can do about it.[15] These forces, be they architectural or infrastructural, shape our decisionscapes in inescapable ways that are barely noticeable, even to the trained eye. Imagine, for example, that you are driving. You may not realize you are driving fast because the road is wide and your gaze is focused on a distant point on the horizon. You may be a driver who cares a great deal about road safety, but you may still find it difficult to keep your speed under control when met with these conditions. Redesigning the environment to manipulate depth cues, though, can correct this error. Many cities, for example, are now using optical illusions on crosswalks, painting them in a way that makes them appear three-dimensional, as though rising out of the ground like ramps or blocks. This causes drivers to slow down in anticipation of a bump ahead.

I have introduced the decisionscape as though it is a new conceit, but humans routinely use space as a kind of overarching metaphor when we describe conceptual relationships between ourselves and the world. At a superficial level, let's go back to the language we use but this time in relation to how we describe our relationships to other people, time, and hypothetical situations. We have *close* friendships and *distant* relatives, we *drift apart* and *stick together*, and we *distance ourselves* from people we don't agree with. The month of September is said to come *after* August (at least in English). And unlikely outcomes have *long* odds. These figures of speech suggest an underlying mental model in which we relate other forms of psychological distance to physical space. Researchers have explored this model with a series of experiments testing how readily we relate other kinds of psychological distance to space and its representations. In one study, participants were shown a series of arrows overlain on an image using one-point linear perspective.[16] Each arrow contained a word and pointed to an area in either the foreground or the background. The words related to different types of distance: social distance, hypothetical distance, or temporal distance. For example, the word *friend* suggests a short social distance while *stranger* suggests a larger social distance. The study used a technique called the Stroop test. The Stroop test uses participant response times in a task to understand the cognitive effort involved in performing that task: the faster the response, the lower the effort. Low effort suggests that the underpinning mental process happens automatically, and we tend to see fast response times when ideas are very closely associated. A classic version of the test has participants reporting the color of the font they see on-screen. The word shown relates to a color that is either congruent with the font color or incongruent. Because participants learn to associate colors with the words that describe them early in life, when they see the word *red* in the color red they show much faster response times than when they see the word *red* in the color green. In this study, the goal was to establish whether we automatically relate different kinds of psychological distance to spatial distance. For example, do we think of the distant future as though it were spatially far away? If this was the case, arrows in the background with words that evoke psychological distance, such as *year*, would elicit a faster response on word recognition than if those same words were shown on an arrow pointing to the foreground. This is exactly what the research showed: we automatically use spatial distance to make sense of our relationships to time, other people, and uncertainty. The ideas of space and distance, in other words, pervade our consciousness, changing our view of the world and our place in it.

The rest of the book explores different aspects of decision-making in relation to the artistic tenets of creating perspective. In part I, I explore the role of *diminution* in psychological distance. Part II addresses the relationship between our *viewpoints* and our decisionscapes. Part III explores the *composition* of our decisionscapes. In part IV, I explore how our environments, culture, language, and conventions impose a *frame* on our decisionscapes. I close the book by looking at how we might find ways to work with the grain of human nature rather than against it, rigging the decisionscape to help us solve our thorniest challenges.

So, without further ado, let's take a trip to the Oval Office.

I DISTANCE AND DIMINUTION

THE OVAL OFFICE, 1981

President Reagan sits in his office. His desk is strangely bare, and the air-conditioning unit hums in the corner, keeping the hot DC summer at bay. He is dressed in his trademark dark suit, a burgundy tie knotted perfectly at his throat. The other man—the one on the far side of the desk—is standing. A panorama plays out in the reflection of a silver water jug: the man on one side, his military uniform grossly magnified by the curve of the metal, and Reagan on the other, a butcher's knife laid out before his hovering fingers.

"So, they are going to attack?" Reagan tries to keep his voice steady, although his heart is beating much too fast.

"Yes, sir. The warhead will launch in the next two hours."

"Then it must be done." He imagines it's nothing more than a script, he is playing a part, someone else's words in his mouth.

"Yes, sir."

Reagan nods, and the uniformed man slowly removes his jacket, as though his control over the motion means something important. Reagan takes the knife and weighs it in his right hand.

"I didn't think it would be so heavy," he says it quietly, reverently.

"You have to push hard, sir, harder than you think."

Reagan nods and stands. The other man removes his shirt and folds it before climbing onto the surgical table that he brought in with him.

Outside, there is nothing but birdsong, the chatter of the aides is gone, everyone is waiting to see if he will follow through. Reagan approaches the man, asks God for help, tries to look the man in the eyes but settles instead for his eyebrows. He feels the knife trembling in his fist as he lowers it to the man's chest, right where he knows the spot is: below the heart and dead in the center of the rib cage.

"Your country thanks you," he says as he raises the blade.

3 BLOOD ON THE WHITE HOUSE CARPET

Before you think about it too much, Ronald Reagan—at least as far as we know—never cut out the heart of an aide in the Oval Office. The story is a dramatization of a thought experiment proposed in 1981 by Roger Fisher, the director of the Harvard Negotiation Project. Professor Fisher's provocation was one part simple, one part ridiculous: to ensure the decision to launch a nuclear strike was properly considered, the initiation codes for the United States' nuclear weapons should be sewn behind the heart of a presidential aide. To access them, the president would have to cut them out.

Fisher's proposal elegantly and outlandishly demonstrates how the decisionscape can be dramatically rearranged by manipulating psychological distance. In both the real and imagined versions of the protocol, the consequences are identical: distant civilians will die if a nuclear missile is launched. It is the *way* the decision to launch is implemented that varies. In the usual protocol, the process is complex and difficult to conceptually connect to the horror of a nuclear strike. It triggers psychological diminution: there is a card with codes, a briefcase, a phone call, and a chain of command that relays the instruction far into the background where, at last, some small and distant figure presses a button that launches a weapon that kills thousands of people. By putting death into the background of the presidential decisionscape, the protocol removes the opportunity for emotional interference. This is, of course, deliberate. A decision as consequential as this cannot, after all, run the risk of being clouded by emotion. But erasing compassion from the calculation is not without its risks. Fisher's version of the protocol corrects for callousness in the most horrific of ways. With the bare-chested aide standing before him, the president "has to look at someone and realize what death is— what an innocent death is. Blood on the White House carpet. It's reality brought home."[1]

The aide also serves another role. He removes any illusion of diffused responsibility that the president may entertain. Of course, in the case of a nuclear strike, it is crystal clear that the president is accountable for what happens, but it may not *feel* that way from the comfort of the White House at the distant end of a chain of command.

Why is it that procedural distance can fool us into feeling our actions are somehow less consequential? To answer this, let's consider another canonical thought experiment: the trolley problem.[2] Take a moment to read it over it and have your response in mind:

There is a runaway trolley hurtling down a railway track. Ahead, on the tracks, five people are tied down, right in the path of the trolley. The good news is that you can do something about it: you are standing beside the track and next to a lever. If you pull this lever, the trolley will switch to a different set of tracks and miss the five people entirely. The bad news is that there is one person tied on this other track and so your action to reroute the trolley would cause it to hit them. You have two options:

1. Do nothing, knowing the trolley will kill the five people on the main track.
2. Pull the lever, knowing the trolley will take the side track and kill one person.

What do you do?

If you're anything like most people, you may have concluded—with much figurative handwringing—that pulling the lever is the right thing to do. (It is worth noting that this interpretation of justice does not cleanly extend to the legal system. While case law is full of exceptions to general rules, in the eyes of the law any intervention, such as pulling the lever, would generally be more punishable than doing nothing.) If you didn't, then you are also not alone: the numbers vary between studies, but about 10 percent of people typically prefer, like you, to take no action.

Now consider a second variation of the problem:

Just like before, the trolley is still on course to hit five people. This time there is no lever. You are standing on a bridge that the trolley will pass under. You know for a fact that pushing something heavy in front of the trolley will stop it in its tracks. There is a man standing on the edge of the bridge who weighs enough to stop the trolley. All you need to do is give him a gentle push. He will certainly die but he will also stop the trolley and save five lives.

Would you push him?

For many people who said they would pull the lever, this modified scenario is literally a bridge too far. In other words, despite
the fact that the consequences of your action are identical in
both scenarios, the mediating role of the lever seems to matter
greatly. Just like the president activating the nuclear codes, the
lever enables us to operate indirectly: we pull a switch that
moves the tracks that reroute the trolley and kill the man.
While the lever allows us to foreground the five lives we are
saving, pushing the man directly to his death foregrounds the
single victim. This switch in our responses suggests two things.
First, we perceive the process by which a result is achieved to
be important, perhaps even as important as the result itself.
Second, we see a distinction between being active and passive
in relation to the death of the innocent bystander; pulling the
lever feels passive, but when it comes to pushing the man, we
feel as though we are actively ending his life. As such, we decide
that it is more morally permissible to do nothing, allowing
the people on the track to die rather than killing the man on
the bridge.

Moral psychologists have explored how we process the
different variants of the trolley problem to try and understand
why our perception differs so greatly. In Joshua Greene's work,
for example, he uses neuroimaging to show that different parts
of our brain are activated in each scenario.[3] When asked if we
would pull the lever, we have a weaker emotional response,
which enables us to engage regions of the brain associated
with logic and rational calculation. When asked if we would
push the man, however, our decision is processed in a region
used for emotive response. Interestingly, these general patterns
of response can be altered. People can be induced to make

decisions focused on the consequences by, variously, solving a logic puzzle right before answering, reasoning through the issue in a second language,[4] or imagining they are advising someone else on what to do. Each of these approaches—approaches we can deploy in more routine decisions where emotion is clouding our judgment—is like antivenom to emotion, neutralizing it with distance, rationalism, or distraction.

Fisher's presidential provocation would have seemed timely in the 1980s, but looking back on it now it also seems prescient. Just as hand-to-hand combat gave way to tanks and planes, long-range missiles have largely ceded to drones. These drones can be controlled from anywhere in the world, from a desk with an ergonomic seat in Arlington, Virginia, to a military exclave in another country's sovereign territory. And they are used extensively. For example, while the numbers are hard to verify, the *New York Times* reported that American drone strikes had killed a minimum of 7,500 civilians in strikes against the Islamic State between 2014 and 2019.[5] Unlike the president, drone operators are protected by a degree of anonymity in that no one would ever know who was controlling a particular drone. Anonymity can also change our appetite for action by adding an extra and impassable layer of distance between ourselves and those who bear the consequences of our actions. A trivial illustration of this can be seen in one variant of the dictator game—a bargaining exercise that only an economist would describe as a "game." In the classic version, participants are assigned to one of two roles: recipient or dictator. The dictator is given some money and told they can split it however they like between themselves and the recipient. There are no penalties for keeping most or all the money, and yet dictators consistently give away a little under 30 percent of the cash.[6] Over the years, the dictator game has been played many times and with many twists. These twists shed light on the conditions that might drive us to give. When dictators know their partner cannot identify them (or that the experimenter will not know how much they chose to give), they tend to keep more of the money for themselves. This finding shows that we need to be vigilant about how people behave when the link between their actions and the consequences is broken. In online environments, for example, people are protected by anonymity, which often leads them to do things they would never dream of doing publicly. Research shows that regular internet users can become trolls just because they are in a bad mood or see others trolling, a sentiment the actor Emily Atack captured brutally in her observation that men "put their daughters to bed, then go online and send me rape threats."[7] In situations like this, a prompt to make people question whether their behavior could, in fact, be traceable can be powerful. For example, one experiment showed that a pop-up reminding people the police can track IP addresses was effective in getting visitors to a web page advertising "barely legal pornography" to exit the site.[8] While these users may not have abandoned the site because the prompts reminded them of their best intentions, the approach was still effective. It brought the potential consequences of their actions into the front of the decisionscape.

Trolley problems and dictator games may seem abstract, but they are increasingly pertinent to our day-to-day lives. Driverless vehicles, for example, need to be programmed with some kind of response to real-life trolley situations. Imagine, for instance, a scenario in which a group of five children runs unexpectedly into the road. The car does not have time to brake, but it can change course and swerve into a concrete wall to the side. If it swerves, the car will kill its adult passenger but save the five children: what should it do? The case of driverless vehicles already shows how much more complex real-world trolley problems are than the original thought experiments. For most people, the fact that the potential victims are children is not a trivial detail, and nor is the fact they actively ran into the road. It is also obvious that, left to their own devices, car manufacturers are unlikely to program their vehicles to kill their drivers, even in extreme circumstances. So, what should we do?

A traditional take on this relatively new problem is to use government powers to establish and mandate the rules on behalf of its people. This is the approach the German government opted for in 2017 when it proposed a set of ethical rules via its Ethics Commission on Automated and Connected Driving. Apart from the question whether governments should be the moral arbiters of such matters, there is a practical limit to trying to establish a fixed set of rules. The complexity of driving is such that it is not possible to program for every eventuality. Instead, driverless vehicles must rely to some extent on machine learning to deal with unfamiliar situations. This means that the car must be able to "infer" what to do over time based on past data and initial inputs on decision principles. These initial inputs *can* include fixed rules for specific scenarios, although they will rarely fit precisely and so they must collectively convey the essence of the principles the machine ought to follow when making its own "decisions." Eventually, perhaps even very soon after these technologies are mainstreamed, vehicles will follow all kinds of courses of action that lead to consequences no programmer or regulator ever foresaw or instructed them on. There will be a full dissection between the algorithm's effects and its creators, leaving us blameless even if we are aghast at the results.

In contrast to the expert-led approach in Germany, others have explored the use of collective consultation: asking the hive mind what the key principles should be. This is an appealing prospect since it gives us the closest semblance to a status quo counterfactual: what would happen on the road if we continued to operate these vehicles with human drivers. This is the approach that MIT's Moral Machine project took.[9] The researchers created a simple game in which participants were asked to make a judgment about what a driverless vehicle should do in a variety of trolley-style scenarios. Each participant played through thirteen scenarios, each detailing an unavoidable accident with two possible outcomes that the participant must choose between. Across the scenarios there are nine central preferences that the researchers test: sparing humans versus animals, staying on course versus swerving, sparing passengers versus pedestrians, sparing more lives versus fewer lives, sparing men versus women, sparing the young versus the elderly, sparing pedestrians who cross legally versus those who jaywalk, sparing those who are fit versus those who are unfit, and sparing those with higher social status versus those with lower social status. Participants provide demographic information and their location to enable a deeper understanding of how preferences vary based on who is responding. The game was a hit, and the final report draws on data from 40 million decisions in ten languages from millions of people in 233 countries and territories. The results provide some helpful global trends but also confirm that there is considerable variation between respondents and across cultures. For example, while there is a strong general preference for saving human lives over those of animals, more lives over fewer, and younger lives over older ones, even these headline rules are not universal. To give one notable exception, people show a slight preference for sparing the lives of dogs over the lives of criminals. (They also prize athletic people over fat people and doctors over executives. Those who are homeless fare poorly. And cats are the least likely to be spared of any "character.") These collective preferences might also disagree with the conclusions of ethicists. For example, in the German government's guidance, it is explicitly stated that factors such as the age of the potential victim should not be considered, an edict with which the average Moral Machine participant clearly disagrees.

The MIT Moral Machine responses don't directly feed into the programming of driverless vehicles, but they do provide a helpful snapshot of our collective preferences for manufacturers, programmers, and policymakers tasked with the ethical design of these machines. But there is no reason to suppose the crowd will land in a humane and fair place on questions like this. In fact, the blur of an average assessment could significantly jeopardize minority groups. If, for example, there are a small number of people in a population with a criminal record and, as the results suggest, most people consider those with records to be less worthy of saving, the crowd will vote to kill ex-convicts with no regard for their personhood. But knowing the will of the crowd is useful nonetheless. In an eerie echo of the unstoppable trolley, there is no brake on the driverless vehicle movement. In the words of the Moral Machine's researchers, "we are going to cross that bridge any time now. . . . Before we allow our cars to make ethical decisions, we need to have a global conversation to express our preferences to the companies that will design moral algorithms, and to the policymakers that will regulate them."[10]

In every example of a moral decision so far, the ethical dilemma at hand has been obvious. But in real life most ethical bear traps do not come neatly labeled. Often the moral implications of taking a particular action are entirely absent in our decisionscapes as they simply do not occur to us. The moral philosopher Peter Singer provocatively illustrates this by asking a simple question: Would you ruin a nice pair of shoes by wading into a pond to save a drowning child?[11] If you answer yes, Singer argues that you should be willing, then, to donate the value of the shoes to a charity focused on saving the lives of children in extreme poverty: they may not be in the pond on your walk into work, but they are still very real and very in need. It is immediately obvious on considering this that most of us could not go through life weighing every financial decision against the opportunity cost of helping starving children. We are wired to tune out the noise of the plight of human suffering. The figurative child in the pond conjures George Eliot's proclamation in *Middlemarch* that "if we had a keen vision and feeling of all ordinary human life, it would be like hearing the grass grow and the squirrel's heart beat, and we should die of that roar which lies on the other side of silence. As it is, the quickest of us walk about well wadded with stupidity."[12] This idea of being "well wadded with stupidity" may sound pejorative, but it hints at a smart evolutionary adaptation. Like all features of our evolution, we can reasonably theorize that being able to distinguish and discriminate between things that are psychologically proximal and distant improves our prospects of survival. For example, imagine you are part of a small band of nomadic humans, perhaps that same group who drew the warty pig on the cave wall in Sulawesi. It is inevitable that you will encounter other animals and even other humans on your travels, all of whom will be competing for the same limited resources to meet the same biological needs. Being able to project out from your own immediate sphere to imagine these other beings, their needs and wants, is critical to survival: if you can't anticipate what might happen during an encounter, you will be unable to prepare for potential conflict. Feats of imagination like this—that is, the ability to transcend our immediate surroundings and context and conceive of a wider world beyond—are a necessary foundation of psychological distance. Just as being able to conceive of distant others or situations is essential, so too is egocentrism. It encourages us to prioritize our most proximal and urgent needs. For example, finding it harder to imagine or empathize with those experiencing a distant famine helps keep me focused on sating my own hunger first. This is a classically crude example, but it gives a simple demonstration of why the ability to create psychological distance might be important. The general principle—a rule that states something like "prioritize things that feel most immediate"—can be deployed in a wide variety of situations with great success. It is a smart and adaptive rule of thumb that helps focus our decisions and actions in day-to-day life. But, like all such heuristics, it is too simple to serve us optimally in every single circumstance.

Singer's experiment also forces us to reckon with the incompatibility between the small locus of our morality and the vast ripples of our actions in a global world. Long ago, when our daily actions had little bearing on people on the other side of the planet, we had far fewer opportunities to save anyone from the figurative pond. Nowadays, though, we live with the uncomfortable knowledge that most of us participate in small acts of harm daily without ever thinking about it: our carbon footprints sprawl, our retirement savings fuel industries that exploit their workers and peddle dangerous products, and our fashion choices sustain child labor. Now our "well wadded stupidity" is far more costly, although its protective value has not changed. More than this, there is a new layer of "wadding" coming our way. Just as globalization put physical distance into our supply chains, new technology—like driverless vehicles—is now creating new kinds of distance in our decisions, often by allowing us to abdicate responsibility for the final judgment.

In 2016, for example, a tool was rolled out across many courts in the United States to help with sentencing and bail decisions. The tool, an algorithm named COMPAS, uses more than a hundred variables, including age, sex, and criminal history, to assign defendants with a score reflecting their risk of reoffending. Those with a score of 5 or more out of the possible 10 points are deemed higher risk and are therefore more likely to be detained while awaiting trial than those with scores of 4 or below. Analysis of the predictions made by the algorithm shows that they are generally good: according to the *Washington Post*, those who are assigned high scores are about four times more likely to reoffend than those with low scores.[13] The problem, though, comes when you look at the false positives—those who were assigned a high score but did not reoffend. Although race is not explicitly considered by the algorithm, this group is disproportionately Black with Black defendants being more than twice as likely as whites to be classified as medium or high risk and thereby treated more punitively by the courts. COMPAS, and similar tools, is still used widely today. Defenders of its use often lay the blame beyond the tool, stating for example that "arrest history" weighs heavy in the prediction and that increased policing in Black neighborhoods means Black defendants are more likely to have been arrested in the past. Similarly, they might argue that the tool is better than a biased human decision-maker or, conversely, that it is merely meant to aid the decision and not replace it. Whatever your beliefs about the suitability of COMPAS, this kind of tool provides a clear example of how technology can reinforce distance. We often discuss the risk of sentient machines turning on us or, more prosaically, the fallout of automating jobs. But public debate rarely turns to the distancing opportunities presented by algorithms. Once the black box takes over, we will be able to wash our hands of all kinds of moral judgments, shrugging our shoulders as the machine "decides" whose life to sacrifice, whether to send someone to prison, or which employees to fire.

The good news is that most of us won't ever be tasked with launching a nuclear strike, stopping a runaway trolley, or programming a driverless vehicle. But all of us encounter moral decisions every day. So, what can we do to hold ourselves to the standard we would like to keep in our best moment?

4 OUT OF SIGHT, OUT OF MIND

Think back to October of 2020. People all over the world had spent months living an isolated life. COVID-19 lockdowns and travel bans meant going months on end without seeing people we loved. Babies were born without being able to meet their extended families. People lived out the last years of their lives alone, unable to even go out to the shops for fear of catching the virus. But as the holiday period neared, it seemed we might finally be able to see our loved ones and celebrate the festive season together. It would, we wishfully imagined, "all be over by Christmas." As time crept on, though, it became harder and harder to ignore that COVID-19 cases, hospitalizations, and deaths were spiraling in many places. In England, the country was locked down again for the month of November in a bid to get things under control. The plans we had made for December seemed less and less sensible, but the idea of disappointing relatives who had been isolated or of deferring our own need to see people until the vaccines were rolled out was hard to stomach. As the same argument played out within families and between friends around the globe, it felt like all of us were living in a cruelly designed ethical experiment. To simplify the decision about whether to meet up, many people shunted the ethical aspects into the distant background where they could be "faded out."[1] They reasoned, for example, that they wouldn't be seeing anyone elderly or clinically vulnerable, without wrestling with the potential of their group to transmit the virus far and wide after the event. Others engaged in what is known as *motivated reasoning*, persuading themselves there was no risk in order to avoid letting down their loved ones: "It's no worse than flu," "I've come straight home after work every day, so it's not like I've been exposed," "Yes, I have a cough, but I just know it's not *that*." Some people were too risk-averse given their personal circumstances, failing to recognize the cost of waiting to see loved ones until everyone was vaccinated. In short, all of us were fighting a losing battle with desires and fears that dominated the foregrounds of our particular decisionscapes.

There is, by now, a large body of research that demonstrates how our rationality and awareness is "bounded"; we don't notice much of the information available to us, and our decisions sometimes suffer because of these blind spots.[2] Just as we all experienced in the dilemma above, this phenomenon also extends to ethical decisions, meaning that we might act in ways that are unethical—sometimes deeply so—without even realizing there was an ethical dimension to the decision.[3] For example, Professor Ting Zhang and colleagues at Harvard ran an experiment in which they showed that students who were instructed to imagine they were fund managers had no hesitation recommending a clearly fraudulent fund to their clients.[4] This wasn't because the students lacked the knowledge to spot the suspicious activity. In fact, when they were asked to declare any suspicions they had about the funds before making their recommendation, they immediately noticed that the fund in question looked highly unusual. While the other funds on offer jumped about with the markets, this one was strangely steady, growing year on year and beating the market time and again. The research seems, on the face of it, like a quirky experiment in a university setting, presumably with limited real-world application. But the kicker is this: the fund in question, and the information accompanying it, was a real feeder fund for the infamous Bernie Madoff Ponzi scheme. In other words, the students were showing the exact same *bounded ethicality* that real financial advisers had suffered from before Madoff was caught.

You would be forgiven for thinking that financial advisers, whose incentives may not be wholly untainted and who are perhaps a little more hard-nosed than the average person, may be predisposed to selectively filter out ethically dubious information. However, bounded ethicality can affect all kinds of people and all kinds of decisions, even ones that explicitly set out to help people. A few years back I was hired to work with a team of social workers to look into a specific issue: Why were so many children being placed in temporary foster accommodation? Temporary accommodation poses two issues. First, temporary placements cannot, by definition, offer a stable home, something that children in foster care desperately need. Second, it costs the government much more to place children in a temporary setting. This doesn't mean that temporary placements should never be used, but it does mean any trend toward using them more frequently is worth interrogating. When I spoke to the social work team, they were also concerned about the trend, but they attributed it to a change in the profile of cases.

They told me about a group of children who had arrived illegally from Europe and needed to be placed fast. They talked about the complex needs of a group of siblings who had to stay together at all costs. And they mentioned the teenager whose recent fascination with arson had caused their foster carers to ask for them to be immediately rehoused. These were compelling stories, but when we looked at the data, there was no evidence of a change in overall case complexity. These kinds of cases had always existed, and they had always posed issues, but they were the exception. Most cases were still simple enough to find an immediate longer-term solution. Next, we looked at the supply side of the equation: maybe there just weren't enough foster homes. Most social workers were easily able to recall examples of experienced foster carers who had recently retired or of families who had settled so well with their foster children that they no longer had any spare capacity. Again, though, when we looked at the data, there was no obvious change in the number, experience, or capacity of the foster carers available.

There was, however, one interesting trend in the data: the use of temporary placements started to increase at almost the exact same time the foster placement social workers were relocated to a new part of the building. They had been moved to sit with a team they needed to work in frequent partnership with: the commissioners. The commissioning team members were not social workers. They were hard-nosed procurement officers, many of whom had commercial backgrounds. They were responsible for the bottom line, and the bottom line agreed it was not good to place children in temporary accommodation. In other words, they had a shared cause with the social workers, albeit for different reasons. Despite this common goal, the teams had not historically collaborated well. The move was something of a Hail Mary: maybe giving them a shared office space would force some camaraderie.

When I sat with the teams to observe how they did their work, it became clear that the move had been very effective. The social workers and the commissioners felt like one team. They went to lunch together, chipped in for birthday cakes, and knew one another's kids and spouses. The relocation, it seemed, had been a tremendous success. But the improvement in team relations was, it turned out, a mixed blessing. When the social workers were alerted to a child in need of a placement, the response process was cumbersome. The system was slow, making it difficult to work out the basic fact of which foster carers had a bed available. When the list was finally generated, the team would use the single office phone line to call each foster family in turn to see if they could take on the new child or children. Calls went unanswered, and those who did pick up were often so overwhelmed by the request that they said no immediately. As the day wore on, the social workers would get visibly stressed that the children would not have a bed for the night. This is when the commissioners would come to the rescue. After all, they had temporary beds in children's homes on speed dial and could easily solve the problem. Time and again they would come through with a solution. The social workers loved them for it, and the commissioners, whose job was usually a thankless back-office affair, felt great. But somewhere along the way, the children and the budget had crept into the background of the decisionscape without anyone noticing.

When we presented this observation back to the team, they were horrified. They immediately recognized the trend we were describing and were aghast that they had not been able to see it for themselves. Together, we turned our attention to how we might fix the problem. The most sensible approach seemed to be to tackle the basic operational problem: making the process of finding a stable foster placement more efficient. We decided to try sending a broadcast text message to all foster carers describing the critical features of the case and asking if they had room. The idea behind this was to quickly reach out to as many options as possible and then follow up with those who responded indicating they had availability. This simple change seemed to be effective, including in ways we had not anticipated. The team typically received many replies and were then able to focus on choosing the best option. The social workers were no longer as stressed, and the commissioners no longer felt like they needed to intervene unless necessary. This solution is pragmatic. It does not try to fix human nature. Instead it sidesteps the issue by designing around it. Often, this is the best way to handle situations where bounded ethicality is at play: it's easier to rewire a process than a human.

Social workers have unusually complex decisionscapes in their professional lives. There are many factors at play, many of which are unpredictable. And the stakes are incredibly high. One bad decision could alter the course of someone's entire life. On another project, one of my interviewees—a social worker responsible for adoption placements—told me that she imagines the child knocking on her door on their eighteenth birthday and telling her they thought she made the wrong decision. "If I feel that, in that scenario, I would still be able to explain why I did what I did," she said, "then I know I am ready to make the recommendation." Another adoption social worker, Katie, allowed me to observe a reflective session with her manager. Together they reviewed the current caseload and the way that Katie had approached each case in the last few weeks. The purpose of "reflective practice" like this is to create a supported timeout where the social worker can think critically about their work and process to improve their approach for next time. Around halfway through the session, the discussion turned to one of Katie's more complex adoption cases: three siblings, all of whom had complex health conditions, and whose birth mother had Jamaican and German heritage. Katie had held the case for weeks with no progress, and her manager suggested she talk through what she was looking for in terms of prospective adopters. Katie rubbed her temples with one hand, covering her eyes as she spoke. "What I am doing here is building up a picture of the ideal adopter. So, it's someone who is used to having lots of kids. Who knows about these specific conditions, how to manage them, how to help with the physio, to do the injections. And they need to be able to give these kids support when it comes to their heritage. So, a German-Jamaican couple. I think it needs to be a couple."

There was a pause in which Katie looked to her manager for reassurance. "And do you think such a family exists?"

Katie laughed. "No, of course not. But I like to set the highest bar, so I know where the match falls short."

Her manager thought for a moment and asked, "And can you think of any reasons why using an impossible bar might make things worse?"

Katie thought for a moment. "It might take me longer to do anything because I am looking for perfect."

Her manager nodded. "What could you do to make the bar more realistic?"

"I don't know, because I don't want to lower my expectations and place them somewhere mediocre."

"And where are they now?"

"In a foster placement."

"And is that a long-term solution?"

"No."

"So could another way to think about placements be to compare options to what happens if they're in the foster system any longer?"

Katie didn't like this idea at first, but after they talked it over, she realized that her standard of an ideal family was also damaging. There was no perfect counterfactual, no German-Jamaican family with experience of these exact medical conditions. But there was a very real counterfactual: the effect of more time in an unstable foster system. By ignoring this real alternative, Katie had run the risk of doing a disservice to the children despite trying to act in their best interests.

This reflective practice session is a great example of how we might improve decisions that really matter by slowing down and dissecting the process behind the decision. When it comes to something as important as deciding where children should be placed for their "forever home," having high standards is no bad thing. But without the tempering influence of structured reflection, high standards—being able to justify a decision to an angry eighteen-year-old or coming as close as possible to the ideal placement—can slow progress and incur a less visible form of damage through delay. Counterfactuals are helpful imaginary devices, but only if you choose the right one. In a scenario like this, time matters too. At some point, one more day in the foster system could be more damaging than an adoption match that is not perfect but is good enough.

Most of us experience the same kind of counterfactual error as Katie on a regular basis, albeit with lower stakes. When we complain about our work or relationships, for example, we often do so as though the things that annoy us are unique to our situation. But there is no alternative job with perfect colleagues, a great office, no commute, generous pay, and the many other things we might take umbrage with. We might also worry that we are underachieving in some way because we can see that we are not perfect. Again, perfection is not a realistic standard and often we only need to be good enough. Many new parents, for example, would be extremely relieved to hear that research suggests you only need to get it right 50 percent of the time when responding to babies' need for attachment to have a positive and long-lasting impact on the baby.[5] This doesn't mean we should all phone it in, and it doesn't mean we should settle when we don't want to. But it does mean we should liberate ourselves from the unhelpful stress of an incorrect counterfactual.

By explicitly describing the alternatives to our current or proposed situation, we might be more likely to catch where we are being idealistic or see blind spots in the decisionscape. But often when we have become blinkered, it is difficult to notice what we are missing, even if we take time out to try. In these situations, especially where the oversights we are likely to make are predictable, external prompts are often more useful than relying on our own judgment. Checklists, for example, have saved thousands of lives over the years by improving surgical outcomes, airplane safety, and skyscraper construction.[6] They work because they are needed in predictable moments, such as right before a surgery is about to begin. Checklists mean you only have to remember one thing—the checklist—rather than everything on it: they make sure each important consideration has its moment in the foreground, alerting you to potential dangers without you ever asking them to.

Building feedback loops into your routines can also help highlight patterns of repeated unhelpful, even harmful, behavior. Feedback loops are effective because they bring the effects of our decisions into the foreground of our decisionscapes. Take, for example, a doctor whose patients keep demanding antibiotics. The doctor is fully aware that prescribing antibiotics unnecessarily contributes to the disastrous rise of drug-resistant bacteria, but they are also faced with much more proximal pressures that cause them to minimize this risk. Perhaps they are just sick of telling agitated patients "no," or perhaps they are worried about overloading the clinic in a few days' time when the patient comes back with no resolution of their symptoms. Whatever the reason, the overprescription of antibiotics is still an issue, and some of it can be traced back to the decisions of individual doctors. However, research led by Michael Hallsworth shows that simply giving feedback to doctors on how their prescribing compares to peers can help reduce excessive prescribing.[7]

So far I have explored how we can overcome issues that arise from too much distance. Broadly, I identified two strategies.

The first is to design around the issue. Change the process, reorder the options, alter the incentives. Basically, it is easier to change the situation than it is to change the person experiencing it. But when we need to confront decisions head-on, or we simply cannot avoid a decision trigger, we can deploy the second approach: pause and reflect. If you are starting a new project, for example, you might set aside time to conduct a premortem. Premortems involve imagining a future time at which you have come to the end of the project and realized that it was an unmitigated disaster. You then try to explain what went wrong and why. Premortems can be a great way to make the abstract idea of the project concrete. More than this, they are a great salve for the overconfidence we often experience at the beginning of a project. Assessments of premortems bear this out. For example, in an exercise involving disaster recovery planning, those who conducted a premortem were much less confident in their plan at the end than those who did not.[8] While underconfidence is not generally a good thing, the right level of confidence helps us adjust our approach to a task effectively. Revising down confidence estimates likely reflects the fact that the participants simply had a better sense of what it would take to succeed.

The next chapter looks through the other end of telescope and asks: How do we overcome the perils of too little distance?

5 "EVERYTHING IN MY FACE ALL THE FREAKING TIME"

Cheri was eighteen months into a two-year role in Investigations when I met her. I was assigned to do a ride out with her: eight hours together covering the area around a city somewhere in the United States South. I could see why I had been paired with Cheri. I had come to town attached to one of the Child Protection Agency's funders, and so it would have seemed important to put me with someone who would make them look good. Cheri was warm, open, and clearly brilliant at her job. She was, and for this I was very grateful, the kind of person I knew would make a summer's day with no air-conditioning as fun as possible.

Investigations is pretty much what it sounds like. Child Protection cases get flagged to a central call center, and the ones that seem especially serious get referred to a team for immediate examination. This team is made up of social workers like Cheri. Each one has around thirty cases at any one time and a period of a week or so to investigate them. There's some desk work—checking people's records on a computer or trying to figure out which other services they are already in contact with, for example—but most of it involves driving to people's houses without an appointment and asking them to let you in so you can, as far as they are concerned, assess whether their kids should be in foster care. I have heard more than once from people in these jobs that you need a flat pair of shoes so you can run and a clipboard that can double as a shield. When I got in the car with Cheri, she said, "I am so glad they sent you today: I've got three places out east that I can't go to alone." And off we went.

The first thing I noticed was the paper. It was all over the backseat and spilling into the center console, piled up and collapsing over itself. Each time a new address flashed up on the bulky laptop Cheri had propped on her dashboard, she would send her right hand back into the mess behind her and grope around until she somehow found the exact part of the pile she was looking for. There were case notes from previous visits, legal papers, and government forms, most of which she had to go into the office before her shift started to print out, she told me. When we arrived at the first house, a woman answered the door almost immediately. She gestured us inside and went over to the sink. She turned on the faucet, just long enough to show us that there was running water, before snapping it off again. Cheri made a check mark on a huge list and thanked her before handing over a plastic tube in a sterile bag. The woman walked to the bathroom and pissed into the tube with the door open. When she was done, Cheri took the tube in the bag and asked her some questions about the children and the man lying on the couch. His forearm was flung over his eyes, but even in the dark of the room, we could see from his breathing that he was awake. There was an old chair, the upholstery torn and gaping open at the back. I sat down, trying to get myself out of the way.

When we got in the car, Cheri told me she would send me a bill if I got fleas or bedbugs on her seats. She was only half joking. It wasn't even nine a.m.

The rest of the morning went fast. We saw a woman whose child's eczema was so infected it had left a brown stain on the mattress they shared. Cheri was already an hour behind schedule at this point, but she helped them fill out a form to get an exemption from the $500 bill for the medication they needed. All the while the little girl scratched at herself through the thick sweater she was wearing. When Cheri asked if she had anything cooler she might put on, the mom whispered that she had no other clothes. Cheri went to the car and took out some kids' shirts. I have no idea where they came from, but it wasn't the office.

Next, we pulled into the driveway of a huge detached house that looked as though it had been washed just for our visit. Before we could ring the bell, the door was opened by a woman who was quick to tell us she had invited her lawyer over just in case we came by. She offered us iced drinks and asked us to take our shoes off. When Cheri asked her to run the faucet, she let it go on for several seconds, bemused at the idea anyone might not have running water. The neighbors, she said, had been mistaken when they had reported seeing her husband beating her teenage son in the yard.

As we ate lunch—a pasta salad from home for Cheri and a hot dog from the 7-Eleven for me—I was eager to review the day so far. After just one morning of observing Cheri's caseload, I felt sad and stressed.

I clumsily asked, "So how do you . . . manage all this?"

"You mean everything in my face all the freaking time?" She laughed. "I just try not to think about it too much, that's my motto. Thinking about it won't make it better."

I asked a few more questions, but Cheri obviously didn't want to have the conversation. She wasn't guarded so much as disengaged from it. As she said, I suppose she didn't want to think about it any more than she had to. We got back in the car, and Cheri drove us "out east," trying and failing to reassure me that we could just leave if anyone pulled a gun. As we parked by the first place, a trailer with a patchwork of faded warning notices from the city behind one of the windows, she asked me if I had been around dogs much. They wouldn't turn on the faucet when she asked, and we didn't stay long after that.

For Cheri and the hundreds of thousands of others doing jobs like hers in the United States, the decisionscape really is "everything in your face all the freaking time." Someone in the governor's office or a federal desk job works at a distance. They think about the big picture, but every small cut they make, every adjustment to the pathways through the system, can have huge repercussions for someone on the front line. Checking there is running water makes a lot of sense on paper, but when you forget because you're too busy planning your exit route it means you have to add a twenty-mile trip to the end of your day to check that box. I've talked about the faucets a lot. Just before we said our goodbyes, Cheri told me that she thinks of them involuntarily before she falls asleep. She laughed, as though she imagined it sounded silly and trivial, but it didn't. It made me think of something called the *Tetris effect*, a phenomenon whereby people who play a lot of Tetris see the blocks falling in front of their eyes as they try to sleep at night.[1] The Tetris effect extends far beyond the realm of retro gaming. When we see the same patterns throughout the day, we find our brain struggles to forget them. Lawyers and auditors might become obsessed with poring over detail, looking for mistakes, for example. In hindsight, Cheri's hypnagogic faucets were a red flag: she couldn't switch her brain off from the unbearable weight of her caseload.

When I emailed Cheri a couple of months later to ask her a question about something, I got an automatic response from the server saying her account was no longer active. When I checked in with her boss, I learned that she had left both the job and the profession. After that I stopped wondering why people burn out in jobs like these and started wondering how anyone manages not to: With no distance whatsoever between your professional decisions and the consequences for people's lives, how do you find ways to cope?

This is the kind of question that motivates Harvard professor Elizabeth Linos and her colleagues at the People Lab. Among other things, the lab studies burnout, a syndrome inducted into the International Classification of Diseases by the World Health Organization in 2019. Burnout results from "chronic workplace stress that has not been successfully managed."[2] Its symptoms include exhaustion, negativity, psychological distance from one's job, and reduced professional efficacy. It is also associated with reductions in creativity and some aspects of executive function. In other words, burnout is bad for workers and bad for employers. Because burnout is caused by unmanaged stress, we tend to think that dealing with it will require investment in improved management and extra capacity to give individual workers more slack. While these investments would certainly help, they are often beyond the budgets of managers or departments looking to help their staff. As such, there is a pressing need to figure out ways to help people in roles like Cheri's without extra investment.

If burnout is partially caused by "everything in my face all the freaking time," as Cheri put it, it is perhaps unsurprising that finding a sense of purpose that brings perspective to your work can help protect against burnout. This may be something you bring to work with you already. For example, some research shows a positive correlation between religious and spiritual beliefs and lower levels of burnout among workers. However, at least in jobs that do inherently have a meaningful purpose, focus on the bigger picture can also be induced through surprisingly simple interventions. One such approach is to make sure that workers are connected to a wider community of people who share their experience. Being connected to others who are doing the same job seems to help give us a sense of perspective and a frame of reference. When someone else shares an experience, it is easy to see how important their actions were. Specifically, you can hold the bigger picture in mind in a way that you cannot in your own crowded decisionscape. This isn't about stuffing everyone into the same office and letting them work side by side. The important part is sharing stories about the common experience.

To see if sharing stories could help prevent burnout, Linos and a small team worked with 911 dispatchers across the United States.[3] 911 dispatchers occupy an unusual professional niche. They are often exposed to traumatic incidents, and their actions can make the difference between life and death, but, because they sit behind a desk, they are generally treated as clerical staff: they might be able to get a wrist support to protect against carpal tunnel, but they're unlikely to get access to counseling services to help with post-traumatic stress. There is another important deficit in their jobs too: status and respect. 911 dispatchers aren't being thanked for their service or told they can board flights before everyone else. They are just seen as regular call center staff. Given that it's difficult to magic up structural support and elevate the status of an entire profession, it seemed unlikely that something as basic as sharing stories could make a meaningful difference for these workers. But it was worth a try. So Linos and her team split the 911 workers into two groups. One group carried on as usual. The other saw a minor change in the rhythm of their week: these dispatchers got an email from their supervisor asking them something like "What would you tell a newbie about what it's like to be a 911 dispatcher?" or "What are the characteristics of a good mentor and who has been a good mentor to you?" The questions changed, but, along with the answers that were also shared with the group, they were all designed to do the same thing: get the 911 dispatchers to reflect on the fact they belong to a wider support network of people just like them. Both groups—those who got the emails and those who didn't—completed follow-up surveys designed to test whether they were experiencing signs of burnout, and all the participating departments shared information on the number of sick days their workers took and whether any of them left the job. The stories made a difference. Resignations dropped by more than half in the group who received the emails, and they scored about eight points lower on the clinical scale that measures burnout. "What that translates to," says Linos, "is approximately the difference between being an administrative assistant versus being a hospital social worker." It costs close to nothing to organize and send these emails, but, at least in the organizations that took part in this study, a city with 100 dispatchers would save more than $170,000 each year if they did something like this; that's equivalent to the cost of three full-time staff.

Even for managers who don't have the time to figure out how to get staff to share their experiences via email, there is often someone in an organization who could if only they were allowed to use their natural superpower. Many years ago, I was working with a local authority struggling with staff engagement. Part of this work involved talking to workers from every one of the hundreds of services run by the council to figure out if there were common stressors. Everyone was stressed, and understandably. The whole council was under enormous cost pressures at the same time as demand for its services was growing dramatically. We weren't equipped to diagnose burnout, but I am pretty sure many of the people I interviewed were experiencing it at some level. One of the hardest teams to find time with was the school-placement team. Their job was to match each year's cohort of children in the area to school places. Parents submit a list of their preferred schools, and this team does their very best to balance the supply of places with the demand for them. It's seasonal work. For much of the year they were dealing with exceptions: finding places for excluded kids, children with additional needs, newcomers to the area, or children who need to move school because of bullying. But from January to April it was a seven-day-a week job matching every four- and eleven-year-old in the area to a school. To make things harder, the population had grown rapidly in the last five years, largely because of an influx of young families. There simply weren't enough school places to make sure every family was happy, and once the places were allocated, the stress of matchmaking was replaced by an onslaught of verbal abuse from angry parents. It seemed almost pointless talking to a team that had no time and were so obviously going to be stressed by circumstance. And then I met Zaynab.

Zaynab was the team leader, who had been described to me by members of the leadership team as "quite difficult," "a lot," and "very passionate, which can be a challenge." When I walked into her office, I was full of dread. I gave my customary apology for taking her time in a very busy period, but she wouldn't hear a word of it. She was warm and enthusiastic and rightly proud of the fact her team had the highest engagement scores in the department, something no one had mentioned while they gave me their scathing briefings. When I asked her to describe her work, she said, "People think it's moving things around in spreadsheets, but my job is setting every child in this borough up for success. Their future rests on what we do." We talked a little about how the team had been very low when she came into the role.

"One thing that I saw right away," she said, "was that they weren't thinking about the point of all this: the end result." So she started trying to show them how important their work was. She asked parents whose problems they solved throughout the year to write thank-you emails to the team. Some sent cards with pictures of their kid in their new school uniform, and Zaynab stuck them on the cheap dividing walls between the desks. She made a progress chart to show the team how much of the job they had already completed. This was a particularly savvy move, as most placements are done automatically with no issues, which means it always looks like you've got a massive head start on the process with minimal effort. She sent an email every week celebrating the resolution of difficult placement challenges as well as other big events going on in the team. And she got the department head to sign thank-you cards for each team member at the end of the placement season.

Zaynab had not gotten her ideas from management books; she seemed to intuitively know how to pull her team's focus to what matters and keep them motivated. But research does support much of what she was doing. For example, some years later I read about an experiment run by professors Adam Grant and David Hoffman to look at what motivates workers.[4] They were trying to figure out how to make fundraisers as effective as possible. The fundraisers made calls to try and drive donations, and so it was possible to measure the number of dollars generated in fundraising by each team member. Grant and Hoffman knew that the team was often given pep talks by leaders, but they wondered if this was the most effective way to get them motivated. Instead, they—like Zaynab—speculated that it might be better to hear directly from someone who has benefited from their work. To this end, the fundraisers were split into groups. Some heard a motivational talk from a leader, and some heard a college student whose scholarship was funded by the donations they generated talk about the impact of the money. The amount each fundraiser generated in donations was then observed over a three-month follow-up period. Those who heard from a leader didn't improve their performance. The student, however, had a huge effect on performance. Fundraisers who heard the student's testimonial almost quadrupled their fundraising, going from an average of $2,459 to $9,705.

In another study by Nicola Bellé, Italian nurses were asked to write endorsements that would be seen by colleagues for a project they were working on.[5] The project was part of an international humanitarian effort to provide medical services and equipment to a former war zone. The hospital in this study oversaw the collection of surgical tools and drugs donated by different organizations, checking their quality, and assembling surgical kits ready for shipment to health practitioners operating in the target area. The activity had to be performed by clinical staff on a voluntary basis outside of normal work hours. By having staff who already volunteered on the project vouch for it, the hope was that more volunteers would lend support. While the campaign was successful in its primary aim, attracting more volunteers, the researchers were also interested in something more unexpected: the effect of writing such an endorsement on the nurses who wrote them. Specifically, could persuading someone else of the benefits of this project improve the motivation and performance of the persuader? Once the nurses had written the endorsements, the researchers followed up to assess the productivity and accuracy of their work assembling surgical kits. Productivity was defined as the average number of surgical kits that each participant completed per minute of work that they contributed to the project. Accuracy was assessed in terms of the percentage of surgical kits that each participant assembled correctly. The results were striking. The act of self-persuasion initiated by writing the endorsement increased productivity by 15 percent while also improving accuracy 30 percent. These results were strongest for those employees who were already motivated. This suggests, fairly intuitively, that self-persuasion might work best when it requires someone to rediscover their passion for their work rather than have to generate motivation from scratch. When we find we have fallen a little out of love with something, we too can write about why we thought it was so great in the first place. It may just be enough to rekindle the flame.

Zaynab and her unusual ability to keep the higher purpose of her work in the crosshairs stuck with me long after that project ended. It wasn't just that she was such a force of positivity, it was the fact that her enthusiasm and vision were seen as irritating to those above her. Surely if your organization has a Zaynab, you should be trying to get her method copied across as many other teams as possible.

Perhaps the leadership's inability to see Zaynab's broader potential was a kind of distance problem of its own. There is ample research demonstrating that our ability to creatively problem-solve can improve when we are working on something that feels more psychologically distant. This is because we think more abstractly, freeing our minds to explore different nonobvious dimensions of a problem. When we fixate on specific details of a problem—in this case, low staff engagement—we become inflexible and incapable of creative thought. Take, for example, the puzzle known as the candle problem, presented as part of an experiment in 1945.[6] Participants are told to affix the candle to the wall using only the materials provided: a box of thumbtacks, some matches, and the candle itself. Take a moment: How would you solve it?

The answer is to fix the box to the wall using the tacks, and then stand the candle in the box. Despite its simplicity, many people fail to solve the puzzle. This is because they experience something called *functional fixedness*. That is, they fail to see that the box might have a function beyond its primary use of storing the tacks. Functional fixedness might affect only one small part of the picture—the box, in this case—but the consequence of this inability to think laterally is that the whole problem becomes unsolvable. In some ways, Zaynab was like the box: she could help with the staff engagement problem—if only those tasked with solving it could see how useful she was.

Overcoming functional fixedness is difficult, especially because most of the time when we encounter it we don't realize that a blind spot on function is the problem. After all, the world isn't full of puzzles where some experimenter knows the answer and we only need to ask to get it. However, research suggests that we can overcome functional fixedness by breaking down the details of a problem into the smallest and simplest parts possible. For the candle problem, breaking the box down reveals it is, variously, cardboard, made of panels, soft, stiff, and sturdy. These features suggest the box could have many uses beyond its role as a container, making it easier to see its potential as a holder for the candle. This approach, known as the *generic parts technique*, works so well that in one experiment people trained in it solved almost 70 percent more puzzles compared to a group asked to solve the puzzles without the benefit of training.

This research into how to increase the odds of creative solutions to problems was developed by postdoctoral researcher Tony McCaffrey. After researching thousands of historical and modern innovations and the "aha" moments that led to their invention, McCaffrey came up with a theory called the Obscure Features Hypothesis.[7] He found that, time and again, innovation relied on identifying an obscure feature of an object and then building a solution based on that feature. In the candle problem, the obscure feature in question is the box's ability to act as a candleholder. The invention of Velcro gives a good insight into how noticing and exploring an obscure feature yields results. In 1941, Swiss electrical engineer George de Mestral took his dog, Milka, on a hunting trip to the Alps. He noticed Milka would end up covered in sticky burdock burrs, or seeds, each day. The burrs were not themselves sticky, but when they hooked onto the natural loops in Milka's fur, they attached firmly. George de Mestral is definitely not the first person to notice that burdock burrs stick to fur. Many dog owners before him will have been irritated by the tedium of picking seeds from a disgruntled dog's coat. But he was the first to see that this property—the ability of the burr's hook structure to attach—could be useful. He spent more than a decade studying and refining the hook-loop mechanism, and in 1955 he filed a patent for Velcro.

This chapter explored the perils of too little psychological distance and how to mitigate them. For example, joining groups with others who share similar experiences to us—be that a profession, a health condition, or a social identity—can help give us perspective when we feel overwhelmed or burned out. There are many such groups online. I, for example, am in an amazing parenting group populated by people with a mutual interest in a specific podcast about serial killers. We share stories, ask for advice, and generally cheer one another on: it's surprisingly wholesome given the nascence!

These things can help us reclaim perspective when we have lost it. But they do so in small ways. The next chapter looks at how our horizons can be stretched farther by asking what it would take to get us focused on the much more distant future.

6 BEYOND THE VANISHING POINT

One day, Honi was walking on the road and saw an old man planting a carob tree. Honi asked the man, "How long will it take for this tree to bear fruit?"

The man replied, "Seventy years."

Honi then asked the man, "And do you think you will live another seventy years and eat the fruit of this tree?"

The man answered, "Perhaps not. However, when I was born into this world, I found many carob trees planted by my father and grandfather. Just as they planted trees for me, I am planting trees for my children and grandchildren so they will be able to eat the fruit of these trees."

—*Babylonian Talmud, Tractate Ta'anit* 23a (with thanks to Dr. Ariella Kristal for sharing)

In the movie *Avengers: Infinity War*, Marvel's finest come together to try and stop Thanos, an evil warlord, from killing half of all life in the universe. Thanos is, unmistakably, the villain and a Very Bad Guy. But assuming we take his Malthusian logic to be true, his reason for downsizing the population of the universe is ostensibly good. Resources are running out, and continued overpopulation will lead to death, suffering, and conflict. Killing half of all life-forms is, by his account, for the greater good. For Thanos, this is not an abstract problem. His home planet, Titan, was destroyed because its leaders did not follow his advice to kill off half their people. In his mind, Thanos is doing the thing no one else dares admit needs to be done. More than this, he is pursuing a fair way to downsize the universe's population. By leaving the decision on who dies down to chance, Thanos's approach does not privilege any one group over another: it doesn't matter if you're Captain America or a regular Joe, your chances of survival are identical. If the universe's population is left unpruned, though, those who are least able to fight for scarce resources will suffer most. In other words, if you're not a member of Team Thanos, you are in favor of death, suffering, and conflict that will disproportionately affect the poorest.

Setting aside the fact that Thanos has a murderous track record, why is it so impossible to endorse his position? Maybe it's another trolley problem: we feel that active intervention is morally inferior to passively letting the disaster play out. But I suspect there's another dimension at play. When Spider-Man, Black Panther, and Groot all turn to dust because of Thanos's actions, we don't see the future generations of life that their deaths protect. Our decisionscapes are focused on the here and now. As such, we can only experience the loss of the thing before our eyes, not of all the possible things that could have been. This is a temporal flavor of the bounded ethicality problem discussed in chapter 4: we fade out the harm our actions will do in the future to justify avoiding pain in the present. To explore this in more detail, let's revisit Peter Singer's thought experiment about the child drowning in the pond. Before, the point was about spatial distance: if you would save a child drowning in front of you at the expense of your nice shoes, then you should pay that amount to save a child far away right now. Now, though, imagine the child is not on the other side of the world: they are distant in time, not space. If the child was going to drown tomorrow, would you ruin the shoes? Certainly. How about next week? Next month? In a hundred years? How distant would the child need to be for us to think their life was no longer worth, say, $250? There is no set answer, but for most of us the weight of the present moment is so strong that we do not need to project out too far into the future for investment to seem worthless.

So we think that the present moment is somehow more important than all the moments that went before it and all that will come after. Our ancestors would have felt the same. When they domesticated crops or built cities or dropped bombs, they would have felt that the new trajectories they set were monumental. Even those of us who lead less exciting lives can't help but be struck from time to time by the sheer improbability of our existence. The chances of being here, now, exactly as we are, are infinitesimal. The uncomfortable truth, though, is that for most people for most of history it hasn't really mattered whether we are alive or not. Without us, even the ones in the history books, the species would still march on. Now, though, as we prepare to move into the second quarter of the first century of this second millennium AD, our sense of importance might actually be appropriate (although this argument could, of course, simply be another manifestation of present bias). Philosopher Derek Parfit describes the modern era as "the hinge of history." "If we act wisely in the next few centuries," he writes, "humanity will survive its most dangerous and decisive period. Our descendants could, if necessary, go elsewhere, spreading through this galaxy."[1] Parfit is not thinking about actions that will pay off in our own lifetimes. He is not even talking about planting figurative trees today for our grandchildren to sit under. In fact, for most of us, the timeline on which advocates of the hinge-of-history hypothesis think is unfathomable. Right now, we are guzzling earth's resources at an alarming rate, catalyzing the collapse of biodiversity, flirting with nuclear and biological warfare, and ushering in an era of drug-resistant bacteria. But these things are medium-term issues; they will be devastating, but even in the most extreme scenario we have Antarctic outposts, bunkers, and submarines for a small number of our species to ride it out in. In fact, the true cost of these events might be one of distraction: by failing to invest enough in prevention, we are ensuring we will need to focus exclusively on threats like these in the future. This means we will not have the time or money available to develop the kinds of technology and plans needed to survive a true existential risk. If an asteroid blots out our atmosphere or a solar flare engulfs the earth, then no bunker will be able to keep the human race from dying out. If we choose now to invest in building a Plan B for humanity, though, we will be able to live out the days between the end of the earth and the Heat Death of the Universe on new planets or aboard vast spaceships.

I must confess that I am far too myopic to get on board with the Longtermism movement—those who advocate spending today's resources solving problems that won't affect us for thousands of generations. Apart from anything else, spending a lifetime on a giant spaceship with Elon Musk's great-grandson sounds a bit shit to me. But I am fascinated by the mindsets of those who can take the long view: why are some people able to invest efforts well beyond the vanishing point of their own decisionscape? Part of this is about natural diversity. Just as hair color varies in a population, so do our temporal preferences. If we all had the same temporal preferences, we would quickly find ourselves in trouble as a species. Too much focus on the future, and the experience of today might be miserable. Too much hedonism, and we would always leave a worse world for our grandchildren. And if everyone lived in the past, we might never change the way we do things. Some mix of these traits, though, brings balance between enjoying the moment, maintaining our traditions and history, and investing in a better world tomorrow. This idea of differing "time perspectives" piqued the interest of social psychology professor Philip Zimbardo. He created the Zimbardo Time Perspective Inventory to help understand individual attitudes toward time and how those individual attitudes compare to population averages.[2] Those who take the sixty-one-question test can be categorized into five different groups based on their attitudes toward the past, present, and future. There are very few people who fit the most extreme description of a given category. Like most things in life, the majority of people have traits from each, but they can still be grouped based on the camp they most strongly identify with. In fact, research into people's ability to balance their time perspectives—that is, to switch their focus between different time horizons as needed—shows that those who can do this effectively are more likely to experience good mental well-being than those who are not.[3] Their decisionscapes are easier to traverse, giving them respite from "everything in their face all the freaking time." Nonetheless, most people's default time preference is the present, and most people who take Zimbardo's test end up classed as "present hedonistic." Present hedonists are risk-takers, driven by a desire to enjoy the good life right now and entirely turned off by planning or enduring any kind of immediate pain that will benefit them in the future. Hot on their heels, though, are the "future-oriented" bunch. These folks are grafters, investing effort today for payoff tomorrow. They will not risk their future gains, and they hate wasting time. To a future-oriented type, looking after their health is important, and if you try to persuade them with emotion, they will counter with probabilistic thinking and logic. Their decisionscapes have minimalist foregrounds and tidy pathways to the horizon. It is easy to see how the right mix of these traits is helpful to a society. The results of this research lead Zimbardo to claim that our attitudes toward time are a critical part of who we are, shaping our decisions and lives.

The time perspective helps us understand what might be going on in the minds of those who are active in the Longtermism movement. Indeed, Zimbardo reserves a special scale for those individuals who score most highly on future orientation: the Transcendental Future Time Perspective.[4] To score highly on this, you must be able to imagine and care about the time between your own death and the end of time. Those whose time horizon edges into the transcendental future are unusually adept at setting aside their present needs in service of tomorrow. Their inner eye gazes steadfastly at the vanishing point, imagining what lies beyond. This means they may be able to motivate themselves to work in a job they hate just to earn as much money as possible in their lifetime. This money can be used to fund innovations that will one day enable the survival of our species. When viewed from the perspective of someone who believes purpose lies on a longer time horizon than the individual lifespan, this extreme act of investment suddenly makes a little more sense.

Despite a resistance to focusing on themselves, people with a transcendental time perspective often seem to make history, even if we don't know their names. Anyone who has ever masterminded a cathedral, for example, knew they would never live to see the walls being finished, let alone its completion. For these architects and for many of those who worked as part of the centuries-long trudge toward completion, piety would have been the driving force. Zimbardo's work confirms that religiosity is linked to being able to take a long view. Cathedrals must also have been an appealing prospect to those who wanted to build beyond their lifetime, as the longevity of the church means they are likely to sustain funding over centuries. But there might also be something about the task of cathedral-building that lends itself to long-term survival. Often, ambitious plans are unrooted in the concrete detail of what it would take to deliver them. This makes sense given what we already know about the link between construal level and psychological distance. Long-term plans are temporally distant, which means we tend to think about them in more abstract terms. This means they may be exciting and motivational, but they are not easily realized, as the steps to progress are not clear. A cathedral must be planned to begin construction. It is also largely plannable in advance. There may be things that need to change on the way—new innovations to benefit from, a different type of wood when a forest gets cut down, or different stone when a quarry falls out of the church's hands—but the bones of the plan remain. Antoni Gaudí, for example, built highly detailed plaster models of the Sagrada Família before he died. The models enabled him to communicate his vision without ambiguity, and his techniques for building them helped him to discover ways to push the boundaries of construction. He would, for example, build huge upside-down models of his buildings, using weights hanging on threads to form the architectural structure. These enormous architectural stalactites enabled him to see how moving one part of the structure would compromise or bolster the other pieces. Over 100 years after Gaudí deployed this technique, construction of the Sagrada Família was stalling. His models had broken, and without them no one could figure out the feats of physics needed to move onto erecting the inside of the building. Eventually, having come up short with architectural software, the architects solved the problem by hacking a program for aeronautical design. The complex physics built into the algorithm were just about enough to reproduce what Gaudí had dreamed up with the most rudimentary tools all those years ago.

Although almost no one has Gaudí's level of talent, we can all learn to make our ambitions more concrete. John Boyd, Zimbardo's coauthor on the book *The Time Paradox*, recalls a study in which the duo worked with young people who had been excluded from mainstream high schools to think about the future more effectively.[5] The approach was simple. At the start of the experiment, Boyd and Zimbardo asked the students to share a dream they had for their lives. The dreams were big. Kids wanted to become rock stars or doctors, for example. Each day, they were asked to figure out something they could do in the future to move closer to achieving this dream. On day one, they were asked what they could do tomorrow. On day two, they were asked what they could do in the next week. The time horizon for their planning slowly edged out as each day passed until the kids were making five-year plans. By starting in the very near-term future, the kids were more easily able to be specific and concrete in what they were going to do. At the start of the study, none of them had any idea how they would achieve their dream. But by the end, the concrete plans they had been prompted to generate helped them see key actions they could take, graduating from high school or reconciling with estranged family members, for example. Anyone can recreate this task to suit their own needs. No matter your dream, planning the steps to get there from today onward, getting bigger and more ambitious as you go, can improve your chances of success.

By understanding that there are different time perspectives that occur at different frequencies within a population and across cultures, it suddenly becomes easier to understand why seemingly simple coordination tasks can be difficult. If, for example, you have a friend who is always punctual and gets angry at you for always being late, you may just have different time perspectives. What matters to him is that he arrives where he is meant to be at the pre-agreed time. What matters to you is that you enjoy the moment, arriving roughly when you're supposed to but not in a way that hurries life away. While this can be incredibly frustrating, having this person in your life could be a blessing. When you have a problem that demands you make a trade-off between today and the future, call that friend. You may not agree with their advice, but it will likely open your mind to a new way of looking at things.

Interestingly, different types of behavioral change strategies might work for those with different time preferences. For example, in a recent study led out of the University of Chicago, Susan Mayer and her collaborators tested whether a range of planning prompts, reminders, and rewards might get parents to read to their children more.[6] This is important, as reading to children at a young age helps their development and sets them up well for academic achievement in later life. But many parents, especially those whose own education levels are lower, do not read to their children regularly. The study showed that these relatively low-cost interventions were effective, more than doubling the time parents spent reading to their children. What is most interesting, though, is that the researchers also collected data on the parents' time perspectives. When they analyzed the effects of the interventions considering this, they found that the parents with the strongest bias toward the present responded most strongly. In other words, giving people who don't naturally tend to plan or value the future tools for planning, reminders to act, and incentives to do so was enough to overcome their present bias.

Differing time perspectives can also explain why groups might consume every resource available, leaving none for tomorrow. It isn't that everyone in the group is individually selfish or that no one cares about the future. Rather, even without having read Zimbardo's work, everyone in the group knows that some group members will have such a strong disregard for the future that they will use all the resources right now with no remorse. If there won't be any left anyway, the majority reason, why not get as much for myself as I can? This problem can be flipped into a solution for structuring the allocation of resources over time. In one study, researchers led by Oliver Hauser explore whether changes to the way a choice was presented could encourage more generous allocation of scarce resources to future generations.[7] In each round of a "game," players were given the choice to extract resources for themselves or to preserve something for the group that played after—the "next generation." When decisions on whether to extract the resource were made individually, the resource was almost always completely depleted with nothing left for the next generation. As I speculated earlier, this outcome was driven by a minority of individuals who extracted far more than what was sustainable. In other words, the destructive tendencies of a small few were making things worse for everyone else. This meant that groups who used a vote to determine resource use did not use up all the resource for themselves. Not only did the binding vote override the small number of people with a tendency to overconsume, it also persuaded those who were on the fence about whether to go all out for themselves to be more considerate of future generations by guaranteeing they will not lose out relative to other players. Such an approach could usefully be deployed in group decisions that require a tradeoff today in favor of sustaining resources for tomorrow.

As we have seen, present bias can compromise individuals and groups. But it can also capture institutions and even whole governments. At least in mature democracies, much of the apparatus of government and politics is not set up in a way to prioritize the long-term future. Election cycles leave a window of only a couple of years between the early days of a new leader and the campaign-focused runup to the next election, with politicians making very different decisions at the start and end of their tenures. Even the annual rhythm of a well-established public service follows predictable temporal patterns that influence behavior. For example, most budgets are set at the beginning of the fiscal year with the expectation they will last until the next. Unspent budgets get absorbed back into the general coffers, and departments that underspend are unlikely to get the same level of funding the next year. Data on US federal government weekly spending shows that this has an interesting effect. Between 2004 and 2009 (the period in which the data were analyzed), federal departments were frugal in the early months of the year, but then found themselves frantically trying to get money out the door, spending almost five times their usual weekly amount in the final week of the year.[8]

It should be clear from the last few chapters that the effect of psychological distance is not inherently good or bad. What is important is that we ensure we are aware of what looms large in the foreground of our decisions and, if necessary, find ways to pay as much attention to the things in the background. Often, this means changing the environment, conditions, or process of the decision. But, as we saw in chapter 5, it can also mean finding ways to remind ourselves in key moments to think about the bigger picture or, conversely, to pay more attention to the neglected detail. One nice way to think about this came from Volodymyr Zelenskyy, the president of Ukraine—a man currently leading a country under attack by its neighbor, Russia. In his inauguration speech to high-ranking Ukrainian officials, he said this: "I don't want my portraits to hang in your offices, because the president is not an icon or an idol. Hang pictures of your children there and look them in the eyes before every decision."

Whether it is our children or any number of other things, each of us is motivated by different things. We see the world through our own individual lenses, coloring our actions and reactions. Part II looks in more detail at how our unique viewpoints change the way we see and navigate our decisionscapes.

II VIEWPOINT

Two men stand on either side of a river. One shouts across to the other, "How do I get to the other side?" Second guy replies, "You are on the other side!"
—Unknown user of r/dadjokes

7 THE WAY I SEE IT . . .

The Centipede was happy quite,
Until a Toad in fun
Said, "Pray, which leg goes after which?"
And worked her mind to such a pitch,
She lay distracted in a ditch
Considering how to run.
—"The Centipede's Dilemma," Katherine Craster (1871)

In the summer of 2021, US gymnast Simone Biles was one of the biggest names at the Tokyo Olympics. Biles is, at the time of writing, the most decorated US gymnast of all time. At the 2021 Games she needed to win four medals—one fewer than she'd taken home from Rio de Janeiro five years earlier—to become the most successful gymnast of all time. But this wasn't the only pressure Biles was under. In 2018, at the age of twenty-one, she had publicly disclosed that she was one of the young gymnasts sexually abused by USA Gymnastics doctor Larry Nassar. The case was already global news, with over 150 women coming forward to tell their own stories of Nassar's abuse. When Biles added her voice to the chorus, it gave, as she knew it would, a new intensity to the media interest in her. In her statement she said, "I have promised myself that my story will be much greater than this and that I will never give up. . . . I won't let one man, and the others that enabled him steal my love and joy."

When the Olympics came, Biles seemed on top form. After a year of COVID-19 shutting down major competitions, she had come back earlier in 2021 and become the first female gymnast to land the sport's most difficult vault: the Yurchenko double pike. But from the first moment in Tokyo, it was clear something was off. In the vault event, Biles fell well short of her usual standard and ended up withdrawing, first from the event and then the whole competition. She said, "I don't trust myself as much anymore. . . . I didn't want to go out and do something stupid and get hurt. . . . It's so big, it's the Olympic Games. At the end of the day we don't want to be carried out of there on a stretcher." Other gymnasts immediately recognized the phenomenon Biles was describing. It was a classic case of the twisties, that same phenomenon described in "The Centipede's Dilemma" poem more than 150 years ago. The twisties go by many names. Some call it choking. For golfers, it's the yips. Archers get target panic, while baseball pitchers live in fear of Steve Blass disease. In darts the specter of dartitis looms at every botched throw. No matter the name, though, each one refers to the simple phenomenon of overthinking something to the point you can no longer perform a familiar task.

Meanwhile in Tokyo, weightlifter Hidilyn Diaz was aiming to win the Philippines's first ever gold medal. Her road to the Games had been tough in different ways than Biles's. After the 2012 Olympics, she had been plagued by injury. In 2019 she had been briefly accused of being an "enemy of the State," part of a plot to oust the Filipino president. Shortly after, she moved to Malaysia with her team to train for the 2020 Olympics. Within a matter of weeks, the COVID-19 virus struck, and they found themselves trapped by government lockdown. Without access to proper facilities she had improvised, fashioning weights from bamboo canes, suitcases, and water bottles. She worked out in a parking space. But despite these challenges, when Diaz arrived in Tokyo she was somehow in the best shape of her life. More than this, her mind was ready. When she stepped up to do her final lift—127 kg, the one that would win her that elusive gold medal—she was entirely in the moment: "I was not thinking of the Olympic record, I was not thinking of a medal; I was just focusing on the movement—one motion, chest out."

Diaz's description is the opposite of the centipede's dilemma. And she is far from the first athlete to remark on the unthinking nature of performance. This sensation of being nothing but movement is part of the phenomenon known as *flow*.[1] Flow, in many ways, is the opposite of the twisties. Athletes in a state of flow are in the moment. They are fully in their bodies, but their minds are oddly detached, so that the experience feels like watching someone else. They report time behaving in strange ways: slowing down, for example, in moments of technical precision and speeding up so there is no room to think. Flow is present in a lot of gold medal performances, and because of this sports psychologists have invested considerable energy in working out how to induce it. In rugby, the New Zealand All Blacks talk about having a "blue head."[2] The player with a blue head is calm, loose, in the moment, able to see patterns of play, and hyperfocused. Red-headed players, on the other hand are ruled by emotions, their egos trip them up, and they lose control of themselves and the game. Golfers have tactical ways to induce such states. For example, players are sometimes told to focus on the club rather than on their own body; the idea is that by putting your attention on something external, you are less able to get in your own way in the crucial moments of the swing. Since the centipede's dilemma stems from being overly introspective, it makes sense that the common theme in its treatments would seek to set one's ego to the side, creating psychological distance to the athlete's advantage. It enables her to detach and step outside of herself to watch the action unfold.

It isn't just athletes that get in their own heads. In an iconic moment of British reality television, for example, the cast of the 2016 *Celebrity Big Brother* were momentarily thrown into a state of awful confusion when a visibly upset Angie Bowie announced to fellow contestant Tiffany Pollard, "You can't say a word . . . David's dead."

Angie was referring to her ex-husband, David Bowie, but Tiffany immediately assumed she was talking about David Gest—another *Big Brother* housemate who had gone for a lie down as he wasn't feeling great. As Angie tries to control a hysterical Tiffany, the other contestants learn the news that "David" has died. They flood into the bedroom to find David Gest peacefully asleep. Tiffany's hysteria turns to anger as she decides Angie has played a horrible joke. In the end the housemates manage to get to the bottom of the confusion. Tiffany is furious, Angie is distraught. And the moment inevitably goes viral. This macabre misunderstanding is a classic case of the phenomenon of *bounded awareness*: two people having the same information—in this case that David Gest was in the house lying down and that David Bowie was Angie Bowie's ex-husband—but only considering select parts of it and failing to see how the other person might be interpreting the situation.[3]

Of course, the deleterious effects of getting out of our own heads raise a larger question: What is this puppet master we call "the self," anyway? It is, famously, a question that many great minds have sought to answer through the ages. Philosophers have dedicated thousands of pages to probing our sense of what it means to be "us." Scientists have taken to the lab to try and identify the essence of a self in various ways. But these approaches have often left us with more questions than answers, and it seems unlikely that it would ever be possible to draw firm conclusions about the elusive nature of being. But for the purposes of understanding our inherent self-centeredness a little better, let's review some of the major themes.

We start in the philosophical realm with a crude overview of two different mental models of selfhood: the Western and the Eastern.[4] In Western societies, the self is individual, immutable, and hermetic. Each of us is a container that holds something we can describe as "myself." We might call it a "soul" or "spirit," or wrestle with the lines between the electric circuitry of the mind and the organic matter of the brain, but we generally share the perception that our consciousness and its unique signature is generated and retained within us. This hermetic self is existentially lonely, so much so that the philosopher Erich Fromm deemed this loneliness the "source of all anxiety."[5] To avoid insanity, as Fromm had it, we spend our lives trying to find connection, be it with one another or with the world around us.

This thirst for connection can lead us to places of deep compassion and care. But it can also lead to acts of collective atrocity. Perhaps this perspective is unsurprising from a Jewish scholar honing his philosophy in interwar Germany. To Fromm, the primal urge to be connected and the deep pain that comes with being isolated explained the social phenomena he saw around him. People submit willingly to authoritarian rule and turn against one another to feel connected to something bigger. To collapse the distance between themselves and their community, they exaggerate the distance between themselves and those they consider to be "other." There is certainly some objective truth to Fromm's idea that existential loneliness imposes a huge toll. Research suggests that the effects of being lonely are vast and devastating, so much so that loneliness is about as harmful as smoking fifteen cigarettes a day in terms of its effect on life expectancy.[6] The effect is driven by worsening physical health. Those experiencing chronic loneliness are more likely to have high blood pressure, greater risks of stroke and coronary heart disease, poorer immunity, and faster cognitive decline. So a lack of perceived human connection is not just emotionally difficult: it literally kills us.

Eastern philosophy presents a different perspective entirely. Ancient Chinese Taoism, a major root of much modern Eastern thought, for example, conceives of the universe and all its beings in terms of interconnected energy. It is fundamentally incompatible with egocentrism, as a truly Taoist perspective would place individuals as part of a larger ecosystem. Those who practice Taoism and its modern offshoots seek to attain transcendence, elevating beyond a bounded sense of self to see the longer span of time and space for what they are. Think back to the different perspective systems adopted in Eastern and Western art. The transcendental quality of parallel projection is a visual representation of this more expansive mindset. These differences in philosophical conception can redraft our decisionscapes, influencing how we behave day-to-day. The ability to delay gratification, for example, varies between Eastern and Western cultures. This mirrors societal values to an extent. In Eastern societies, or at least a caricature of them, resisting immediate temptation, thinking of the collective before the individual, and contextualizing your own existence in the wider scheme of the universe are all celebrated. The corollary caricature of Western cultures is individualistic, nearsighted, and chronically urgent in comparison.

When it comes to delaying gratification, those who have been steeped in cultures that take a long view should be less likely to choose immediate gains over larger longer-term benefits. This is exactly what research with Korean and American subjects shows.[7] When presented with an "intertemporal choice"—that is, the option to receive a small payout now or a larger one in two weeks—Korean participants were able to delay gratification in a way that Americans were not. The researchers also looked deeper to see how the brain itself processes a decision like this. It turns out that norms and beliefs are not purely external. Functional magnetic resonance imaging (fMRI) of brain activity showed what was going on under the surface. For the Americans presented with a choice of a small payment immediately versus a larger payment in the future, a part of their brain associated with rewards fired up, making it hard for them to defer gratification. The Korean participants, in comparison, showed much less activity in this area. In other words, their brains were supporting them in delaying gratification. These differences in our most fundamental selves even have implications for how we treat medical conditions. For example, Western models of psychiatry, such as cognitive behavioral therapy (CBT), provide an individualistic approach to treating anxiety and depression. They seek to help the patient rewire patterns of thinking and examine the relationship between how they process thoughts, how they behave, and how they feel. For someone with a more Eastern outlook who does not see themselves as disconnected from the wider context in which they exist, however, an individualistic approach may be ineffective. In fact, analysis by Ting Kin Ng and Daniel Fu Keung Wong shows that a culturally calibrated version of CBT—Chinese Taoist cognitive therapy—is more effective than the unadapted version at treating depression among Chinese adults.[8] This adapted approach combines Western models of talking therapies with the philosophical teachings of Taoism.

Until fairly recently, at least compared to the timeline of philosophy, it was hard to augment or test any of our ideas about selfhood in a more scientific way. Modern developments in brain scanning, such as the development of fMRI, allow us to study changes in blood flow and electrical signals in the brain when we are exposed to different psychological stimuli. They can tell us which parts of the brain are most active under different conditions, which parts "go dark," and which parts rarely switch off. These techniques allowed scientists to identify something called the *default mode* of brain function.[9] This default mode consists of interacting brain regions that run in the background while we are at rest. This means it is "on" when we are in a state of introspection—for example, when we allow our mind to wander to imagine the future, remember the past, or even ruminate on recurring thoughts. These discoveries hinted at a hypothesis: the default mode brain is the engine room for this thing we call the self. Cross-cultural comparisons also hint at a physiological corollary for the wider locus of selfhood in collectivist cultures. Among Chinese research participants, whose culture typically involves high levels of social interdependence, for example, the default mode brain remains activated when thinking about family members, such as the subject's mother.[10] This suggests that the philosophical conceptions of selfhood in such cultures might translate into a more expansive experience of selfhood at the deepest level.

To test the hypothesis that the default mode network is the physical location of something like a self, researchers needed to find a way to dial down our sense of self. This process of ego suppression seems difficult given the inherently self-centered way in which we view the world, although there are some fairly reliable ways to induce it. Fasting, transcendental meditation, or even some types of psychosis all result in a feeling of ego dissolution, for example. A much cheaper, faster, and more widely accessible way of going about this, though, is to give research participants a controlled dose of psychedelic drugs. Lysergic acid diethylamide (LSD) changes the way the brain operates. Areas that usually work in synchrony—like the default mode brain—stop firing together, while areas that rarely communicate with one another suddenly connect. The visual cortex, especially, starts networking with regions of the brain it rarely interacts with.[11] These two phenomena—increased connectivity with the visual cortex and disruption to habitual neural firing—are responsible for two hallmark features of LSD trips:

hallucination and a sense of, in the words of Aldous Huxley, "solidarity with the universe."[12] This second process, known as ego dissolution, breaks our sense of a boundary between "us" and "not us." It literally removes the sense that we are distinct and therefore distant from the physical and social world we inhabit. Our decisionscapes transform, moving into something like parallel projection, so we can see more things than we could from a fixed vantage point. This transformation of perspective seems to be why psychedelics work as treatments for some mental illnesses.[13] In persistent depression and post-traumatic stress responses, the brain gets locked into a specific circuit of thoughts. Round and round it goes, replaying the same events or repeating the same negative mantras. The more the circuit runs, the more these ruminations become automatic. A drug like LSD disrupts the circuit because it breaks the automatic firing of those neurons. LSD, in other words, can chemically induce a change of perspective. By looking at their fMRI scans at the exact moment study participants report the sensation of ego dissolution, the smoking gun of selfhood is revealed: the default mode brain goes dark.[14]

The fact that we can "switch off" the cognitive processes that enable our sense of self is a little scary. But it also presents opportunities. If we can reliably dissolve our sense of ego, and with it the distance we perceive between ourselves and the world around us, then we might stand a better chance of overriding unhelpful self-interest. Of course, dropping acid every time we need to make a big judgment call is highly impractical, not to mention risky, but the extreme effects of psychedelics hint that there might be more low key ways to dial up the selflessness when we think it might be beneficial. For example, what if we simply changed the stories we told ourselves so we were no longer cast as the main character? James Pennebaker from the University of Texas at Austin identified an interesting way that a shift in narrative happens: small but subtle changes in the pronouns we use.[15] By looking at how people use pronouns when they talk, write, or otherwise express themselves, Pennebaker has been able to predict a whole range of other things about a person with surprising accuracy. Take, for example, someone who has experienced a traumatic event. To begin with, it is likely their account will be dominated by first-person pronouns: this is, after all, something that happened to them being told from their perspective. As time passes, though, that tethering of the event back to the individual becomes unhelpful. It leads to rumination, a painful echo of the centipede's dilemma. When people begin to heal from difficult experiences, they tend to shift the perspective of the story they tell. They use fewer first-person pronouns—I, me, my—and move focus toward the facts of the situation and even the perspectives of others. Pennebaker's research also explores whether written reflection can have curative power when it comes to trauma. To do this, he has conducted several studies using a technique called *expressive writing*.[16] These studies involve writing about something difficult or traumatic, usually for around twenty minutes, without stopping. It doesn't matter if the writing is coherent or legible. There is no obligation or need to show it to anyone else or even to read it back. The exercise is just about exploring your subject through writing about it. The results show profound positive effects on the writer: students get better grades, those who have been laid off find work sooner, and those who take part even seem to have an improved immune response to viruses. Analyzing the writing also shows that same telltale sign of progress: the number of first-person pronouns diminishes as people process their challenges.

When I first came across expressive writing, I thought it sounded interesting but, frankly, ludicrous. The idea that it could be implemented at any kind of scale and that grown adults could be compelled to write about their experiences seemed a fantasy. However, I soon had the opportunity to see if my skepticism was warranted. In 2013, just as I was about to start a new government job, unemployment rates in the United Kingdom were the highest they had been in close to two decades. The combined effect of the financial crisis of 2007 and the increased automation of manual jobs meant that most segments of the labor market were under pressure. It was in this context that the Minister for Employment asked my soon-to-be colleagues at the Behavioural Insights Team—a government unit set up to design policy in line with research on how people actually act and make decisions—for help. By the time I arrived on the scene, my colleagues had already spent several months studying the experiences, actions, and attitudes of people using unemployment services in the UK, as well as the process they went through and the role of their job coaches. Together with Jobcentre colleagues, they had designed and piloted a program that addressed needs the service was not currently designed to meet, including the fact that people who are seeking work often don't feel good about themselves. This program included an optional expressive writing exercise to help job seekers. If I—an unashamed behavioral science fangirl—was skeptical about expressive writing, you can imagine the reaction of the managers being asked to help roll this out to their staff in the

Jobcentres. Luckily for the job seekers, though, one of the managers, Hayley, suggested a simple test that saved the idea from rejection.

Hayley had gotten to know a particularly tricky customer over the course of many months. He was the kind of guy who explained why the furniture was bolted to the floor. In some of the Jobcentres we worked in, there was something called the "green pen" protocol. In the absence of panic buttons or a discreet way of alerting security, job coaches would ask a colleague for a green pen to signal that they should get help: Mr. Jones (a pseudonym) was a green-pen kind of customer, and he wasn't having any of anyone's shit. And so Mr. Jones became our test case. If he was willing to give expressive writing a go, said Hayley, then she would be happy to go out to bat for it. To everyone's surprise, not only did Mr. Jones say yes, he completed the exercise multiple times and gave glowing reviews of his experience writing down his feelings. The writing helped him get his thoughts organized on things that had been stressing him out: an access issue with his child, a relationship that had left him feeling hurt, and the barriers he thought were insurmountable standing between him and a job. We won't ever know if the expressive writing helped (although I'd bet good money that Hayley certainly did), but not long after Mr. Jones stopped coming into the Jobcentre: he got himself a job. When I trained the staff who would be responsible for asking their clients to do some expressive writing, Mr. Jones's story was more compelling than any research paper. Many of the staff tried the exercise for themselves and came back with stories about how cathartic they found it. It was as though they were able to take the worries that dominated the foreground of their decisionscape, ball them up, and throw them into the distance. Crucially, the exercise seemed to work: job seekers who were introduced to expressive writing—as well as a bundle of other changes to the way the process of looking for work operated—found work faster than those who went through the standard process.[17]

This chapter has explored the ideas of egocentrism and self. Just as our field of vision is limited by the shape of our eyes, our decisionscapes are limited by what we can see from our fixed vantage points, and distance is always defined in relation to us, the viewer. But, as we have seen, there are ways we can challenge this fixedness, even if we cannot overcome it entirely. At the extreme we can learn to meditate, immerse ourselves in a different cultural worldview, or drop acid. More accessibly, perhaps, we can write about our struggles and problems and experiment with different ways to frame and tell our stories. The next chapter digs deeper into what shapes and changes our perspectives and how we can overcome the forces that threaten to derail us.

8   THE VEIL AND THE LENS

In 2017, some colleagues and I worked alongside the International Rescue Committee, a charity that runs the education services in the world's third-largest refugee camp, Nyarugusu, in Tanzania. Nyarugusu is home to around 150,000 refugees from neighboring Burundi and the Democratic Republic of the Congo. When people think of refugee camps, they tend to imagine temporary settlements, places that people cycle through right after fleeing conflict or persecution. But for many of its inhabitants, Nyarugusu is home. There are adults who were born there, and many generations of some families who live side by side. It has markets and hairdressers, a radio station, savings groups, and sports teams. The children go to school, and there is a hospital on site. In many ways, Nyarugusu is like any other large town.

Most people who arrive in Nyarugusu, though, are fleeing violence that would be unimaginable for most people reading this. Without resources, many have had to pay a high price to make it safely to the gates. Some of the young girls in the camp, for example, were promised in marriage to predatory traffickers as babies in exchange for ferrying the family to safety. Their relatives wait for them outside school to be sure they will not be "claimed" on the way home. I give this detail to show that violence is a constant in this world. Almost everyone has been a victim of violence, and the cycle continues each day. In schools, corporal punishment is as much a part of the classroom experience as the sound of chalk on a board. Children are beaten with sticks, made to hang upside down, forced to walk on their knees across sharp gravel, and made to clean the toilets, which can make them extremely sick.

It was in this context that we arrived in Nyarugusu as part of a project team focused on reducing corporal punishment in the camp's school. We interviewed teachers, sat in on classrooms, and spoke to children. Two things quickly became clear. First, with some exceptions, the teachers genuinely wanted to teach the kids and took their responsibility to educate them seriously. Second, they saw corporal punishment as a core part of that job. Many of them have classrooms with fifty or more children. Without the fear of being beaten, they say, it would be chaos. Having seen some of the classrooms, it's hard not to see where they are coming from. When we asked them if they thought physical punishment had any negative effects on children, most of them said no. In general, there was a view that so long as you didn't leave a mark, it was a perfectly acceptable form of discipline. One even invoked the Bible: "Whoever spares the rod hates his son, but he who loves him is diligent to discipline him."

With these insights, we started looking at what we could do to reduce support for violence and pave the way for training the teachers in other forms of discipline. We wondered whether we could tap into the teachers' keenness to nurture the children and use it to persuade them that corporal punishment is harmful. To do this, we designed a simple experiment. Teachers were paid to take a short survey to help us collect more data on attitudes toward violence. While the data from the survey would be useful in itself, we were interested in how changing the information they saw right before completing it would change their answers when it came to supporting corporal punishment. Some of the teachers read extracts from the official guidance for teachers in the camp. This guidance, which was familiar to all the teachers, was based on the United Nations Convention on the Rights of the Child, the most widely ratified human rights charter in history. It outlined the official rules of the camp and explicitly forbade corporal punishment. Documents like it are used all over the world to guide those in official positions of power in their work with children. A second group was given information on the clinical effects of beating children. Specifically, they were told about the long-lasting negative consequences for development and shown brain scans of children who had experienced violence compared to those who had not. The third group of teachers were asked to reflect on their own experiences as children and then shown stories from students about how corporal punishment had affected them. They were then asked to imagine what it must feel like for those students.

When we analyzed the answers to the survey, we found something interesting. Both the clinical information and the perspective-taking exercises reduced support for violence. The clinical information corrected a misunderstanding by showing that corporal punishment can have long-run negative effects.

The perspective-taking exercise, though, simply helped teachers to see the story from a different angle by putting them in their students' shoes. As such, we might have expected this approach to be less effective, but the reduced support for violence among the teachers who had done the perspective-taking exercise was much more marked than for the teachers who were given the clinical information. After completing the perspective-taking, teachers were 31 percent less likely to agree that violence was a necessary and acceptable part of the job and 26 percent less likely to say violence was acceptable in specific scenarios. For the clinical information group, the reductions were 15 percent for each measure.

Of course, sometimes no amount of perspective-taking is likely to work. It doesn't matter if the action is in someone else's interests if it's against your own. In these cases, we need to find ways to structure the decision itself in such a way that mitigates against the warping forces of self-interest. One way to do this comes from a thought experiment proposed by the philosopher John Rawls in the 1970s.[1] Rawls wanted to find a way to get a group of people to make individual decisions that would coalesce on the most just outcome for the group even if it was at the cost of some individual gains. There are many real-world decisions like this. Some are trivial, for example, trying to organize an overnight trip for a group of friends who all have different needs and preferences. Some are more consequential, for example, designing a taxation system that rewards hard work but also redistributes enough money to look after those who need extra support. To do this, Rawls imagined that the individual decision-makers knew what the effect of their decisions would be on people in different social positions but had no idea of their own social standing or personal circumstances. That is, they had to make decisions about how to allocate group resources without knowing if they were wealthy, in good health, part of a minority, or any other facet of their situation that might alter their windfall from a community allocation. This "veil of ignorance," as Rawls put it, was intended to short-circuit the inevitably self-interested motives driving individual decisions. It ought to work particularly well in settings where the poor vastly outnumber the rich but the rich typically make decisions on behalf of everyone else. The theory was that—given the risk they might be the poorest member of the group without knowing it—individuals would become more just in their decisions, solving for fairer allocation, and ensuring a minimum level of payout for everyone in the group.

Experiments that ask people to make decisions under the veil of ignorance bear this out. For example, in one study participants were asked to decide whether autonomous vehicles should be programmed to reduce loss of life, even if that meant killing those in the car to save inattentive pedestrians.[2] In the specific scenario, there were nine pedestrians and one passenger in the vehicle. In the experiment, some participants were asked, "Is it morally acceptable for a state law to require autonomous vehicles to swerve in such a situation to save the nine pedestrians?" The other participants were given a veil of ignorance by being told to imagine they had a 9 in 10 chance of being a pedestrian and a 1 in 10 chance of being the passenger before being asked, "Please respond from a purely self-interested perspective: Would you want to be in a state where the law requires autonomous vehicles to swerve in such a situation?" Under the veil of ignorance, 83 percent of participants favored killing the driver compared to 58 percent of participants who were deciding without the veil of ignorance.

Although the veil of ignorance experiment is hard to apply in real life, aspects of it can be modified with great effect. For example, in marketplaces where some people are more likely to be discriminated against than others, limiting the information shared in a transaction can be a powerful way to force equity. For example, people of color are penalized by other users on the online property rental platform Airbnb when their identities are shown on their profile. In a series of research papers, Asian and Hispanic hosts in San Francisco are shown to have listings more than 9 percent cheaper than their white neighbors, and prospective guests are 16 percent less likely to be accepted by a host if they have a distinctively African American name.[3] To try and reduce discrimination based on race or ethnicity, Airbnb now keeps profile pictures blank until a booking has been made. This mirrors an increasingly common trend in recruitment where résumés are edited to only show critical information until the point at which an initial decision on whether to interview the candidate has been made. This movement was triggered by another wave of studies known as CV audits. These studies involve sending applications to a range of open jobs using the exact same résumé but a different name or photograph. They typically measure the number of callbacks the various fictional candidates receive to quantify the level of discrimination in the market. These studies have shown that Emily and Greg, traditionally white names, receive 50 percent more callbacks than Lakisha and Jamal,[4] that Adam gets three times more interviews than Mohammed,[5] and that—at least in

Norway, Iceland, and Sweden—female applicants to associate professor jobs are deemed more competent and hirable than male applicants with an identical CV.[6] Many organizations are now using specialist hiring software to remove discriminatory decisions from the initial stages of their hiring processes. This seems to work. Using data collected across thousands of its recruitments, the blind-hiring firm Applied has reported dramatic changes in who gets hired through its process. Specifically, its own experiments show that 60 percent of hires would be rejected based on a regular CV-screening exercise.[7]

These studies speak to something important. The egocentricity of our decisionscapes is not just about the angle we are looking at things from. It is also about our identities, the lens we see the world through: our decisionscape is shaped by who we are, not just where we are standing. Some of this is fixed, but much of who we are, who we think we are, flexes and moves over time. This is especially true in a world where each of us sees a different cut of the vast amount of information available. Our varied media diets means that over time we are, based on our preferences, exposed to some messages much more than others. In the United Kingdom, for example, the *Sun*, the country's most popular newspaper, has very little readership in the city of Liverpool owing to a widespread boycott that started in 1989. During the 2016 Brexit referendum, the *Sun* supported the campaign to leave the European Union. Across the country, communities with a similar economic and demographic profile to Liverpool came out in favor of "leave." In Liverpool, though, 58 percent of voters chose "remain," likely because they had not been exposed to the Eurosceptic coverage of the *Sun*.[8] Similarly, a US study shows that switching from Fox News to CNN was enough to shift the political views of subjects in an experiment by changing their factual beliefs, attitudes, and perceptions of issues' importance.[9] As technology develops, the potential threat to democracy is exacerbated by increasingly smart algorithms (a phenomenon trivially highlighted by a friend of mine who said, "I don't get why TikTok is so popular: it's just Microsoft Excel videos"). I was familiar with this growing body of research, but it came to light for me on the runway at Cairo airport in November 2016. We had just touched down after a bumpy overnight flight from New York. When we left, around nine p.m. East Coast time, the votes for the presidential election were still being cast. Hillary Clinton, according to the polls, had been given a 95 percent chance of winning. As I waited for my phone to find a signal, three women in the row behind me began to chatter excitedly in a mix of English and Arabic. I turned in my seat and asked, "Did she win?"

"He won!" one of the women said. She was clearly elated. I assumed she was joking.

"You wanted *her*?" said another. The three of them looked bemused.

I found just enough brain power to ask, "You wanted *him*?"

The women laughed, which was good of them because I was being pretty rude at this point. The two who had spoken wore hijabs and had accents that sounded like they were in the cast of *Jersey Shore*. It seemed impossible that they could be rooting for Donald Trump, the guy who openly flirted with the idea of a Muslim registry, who clearly didn't think of them as true Americans.

"The Clintons started ISIS," the third woman said.

I felt as though the back of my scalp was shrinking as those words sunk in. I turned back and watched the messages coming in on my phone.

The night I got back to the United States, I decided to do my own version of the experiment where Fox viewers were switched to CNN. I wanted to understand what information other people were seeing and how it might have led to an election result that took me and most people I knew entirely by surprise. I unfollowed everything on my Facebook and replaced them with right-wing media sources, like Fox and various pro-Trump groups. When I woke up the next morning, jet-lagged at 4:00 a.m., it was like I was living in a different world. Overnight my entire timeline had been replaced with an unrecognizable set of opinions. It was as if there were different versions of reality all being run at once, a set of quantum truths that you could jump between using only social media algorithms. Within a couple of days, I had seen a whole new side of the debates I was so used to consuming, and a lot of it made me think hard, not about why those who watch Fox hold their beliefs but why I am so sure mine are less biased.

This kind of perspective taking is clearly helpful and healthy. Each of us could stand to entertain the other side of a debate to make sure we are really interrogating our own biases. Research backs this up.[10] In debate competitions, participants are randomly assigned to represent one side of an argument. In other words, their prior beliefs are not taken into consideration, and they are often tasked with arguing for something they do not agree with. Since the purpose of the exercise is to construct a better line of argument than the opponent, it is not necessary for the debater to believe their position to win. However, by the end of a debate, participants typically endorse the viewpoint they are advocating, believing it to be more factually robust than the opposing stance. By spending time constructing and performing arguments for something, we come to believe it. To get balance, all of us need to spend time with "the other side."

In my Facebook experiment, joining the first set of groups seemed to give me some kind of digital passport into the fringes of a much darker section of the informal media. By clicking "join" to the next group suggested and the one after, I soon found myself in the company of conspiracy theorists, white supremacists, the alt-right, and self-identified male rights activists. These groups were (most of them have been shut down following changes to the platform) united, in the most part, by hatred of common enemies. At first glance, these groups exist to share information that serves their cause and might be "suppressed" elsewhere. But their primary function is not about information at all: it is about community. In the day-to-day back and forth of a white supremacist group, for example, I saw the following exchange between a high school senior and some older men:

> **Member 1:** Fuck this shit im done. Been kicked out for two weeks for calling some shithead n****r what he is. School fuckin SUCKS.
>
> **Member 2:** Hey man sorry to hear that. Ignore those assholes. But don't give up on school k? I didn't graduate because I quit. Wish I could go back. Finishing high school gets you places. Don't let this n****r ruin your life.
>
> **Member 1:** Thanks man, but its to late for me. I hate them all. I cant go back.

Member 2: We are all here for you Member 1. Seriously take the two weeks to study, then go back and take their dumb tests and prove them your not who they think.

Member 1: I hate it there.

Member 2: I get you. I hated it. All the kids thought they could start something just because i said the truth. The teachers would ignore it. Public education is a joke. They teach these kids every day and wont admit whats obvious about this country. Your not going to let them win. Promise me you go back.

Member 1: Sounds like my High School. I will try.

Member 2: Member 1, imma kick your ass myself if you don't go back in there! We got you, son. Don't let them take your future.

Member 3: What he said, bro.

Member 1: Thanks. If i didnt have you all i wouldnt be here ha

Member 2: We love you, man.

These were not nice people, but here they were doing a nice thing for one of their own. This was not unusual: in this group united in hate, there were fiercely protective and caring bonds between members. Most of the group members were, by their own telling, misfits in wider society. This nasty corner of the internet was, to them, a sanctuary. In among the racist memes and error-littered articles, I saw one guy step in to pay another's fees so he could get his car back when it was impounded. When someone posted a photo of himself and his daughter at a purity ball, the comments were oddly wholesome. I share these stories not to minimize the abhorrent views of these groups but to reinforce the point that our identities are complex and each of us has many different versions of ourselves depending on the context. Someone might be an American, a football fan, a brother, an accountant, white, male. These social identities collectively govern the way we see the world and the way the world sees us. Sometimes one identity is more salient than another, shifting the angle from which we view our decisionscape. For example, in a work presentation your professional identity is activated while your role as the captain of your neighborhood basketball team is pushed into the background. This is something that can be induced or manipulated. In classrooms in the United States, Hunter Gehlbach and colleagues conducted an experiment with 315 ninth graders and their twenty-five teachers to see if drawing attention to a shared identity could help improve outcomes for minority students—that is, those students with whom the teacher did not share an obvious and dominant social identity.[11] The experiment was simple: students and teachers filled out a questionnaire on seemingly trivial aspects of their life and preferences. They answered multiple choice questions like "If you could go to a sporting event, which would you go to?" and "What is the most important quality in a friend?" The answers were then matched, and, for around half of their students, the teachers were told five things they had in common. When the researchers followed up, they found that teachers thought they had better relationships with those students with whom they knew they had something in common. More importantly, this translated into the kids getting better grades. The effect was most pronounced for kids who were underserved. In this context that was Black and Latino kids who, compared to their white and Asian classmates, typically faced more challenges at home, in school, and in their communities. For this group, the improvement in their course grades closed more than 60 percent of the achievement gap with their well-served peers.

Our social identities and the ways we behave change over time too. We might marry, become parents, get new jobs, retire, and experience a host of other life events. Many businesses are switched on to this and use it to their advantage. For example, some supermarkets place heavy bets on new parents not having time to shop around. This bet comes in the form of an extensive, quality, and incredibly cheap range of baby products. These products are loss leaders, sold below their market value with the knowledge that they will act as a hook to lure new parents into the store. This is lucrative because parents buy a lot of other things and remain loyal customers long beyond the short time their babies are in diapers. Beyond the commercial sphere, though, changes also allow us to reimagine ourselves. When we move house, for example, we are momentarily freed from our old routine and have a window of opportunity when we could become the kind of person who, say, bikes to work. In Portland, Oregon, some colleagues and I ran an experiment with the city transportation bureau to see if we could increase use of the city's bike-share initiative.[12] We sent promotional offers to two different types of residents: those who had one of the new bike-share stations close to their house, and those who had newly moved to an area with a bike-share station. Of course, there may be fundamental differences between these two groups, but on paper at least they looked similar enough. When we looked at the take-up of the offer, we saw a large difference between the groups. Those who had recently moved close to a bike-share station were almost four times as likely to have taken up the offer than those with a new station built near their existing home. Moments of change are powerful: they give us a brief window when our social identities are in flux, and that can be used to our advantage.

This chapter described how our interests, identities, and circumstances shape our decisionscapes. But we do not exist in a vacuum. Other people exert huge influence over us. This is the focus of the next chapter.

9 EVERYONE ELSE JUMPED OFF A CLIFF

Changes in where we live or how we spend our days can also alter who influences us. So much of our behavior is shaped by those around us that changing our social environments can fundamentally shift how we see the world and how we behave, like some kind of identity dialysis. To give a twee example, consider my father-in-law's puppies. For several decades, he has consistently owned two dogs: a West Highland terrier and a Norwegian elkhound. Westies are small, elkhounds are big, but, crucially, it seems neither can deduce its own stature. You see, each generation of dogs alternates between a small Westie raised by a large elkhound and a large elkhound raised by a small Westie. The result is quite remarkable. While the dogs display classic characteristics of their breed, such as barking at noises in the woods (the elkhound) or chasing small animals (the Westie), they also adopt behaviors that might be better suited to the alpha dog they grow up with. Specifically, they seem to imagine that they must be built the same as their big brother: elkhounds stop at walls they could easily step over, flummoxed as to how to conquer such a huge obstacle. The tiny Westies, meanwhile, see that same wall and leap headlong into it, baffled and a little abashed that their enormous stature does not seem to help them pass.

We humans, of course, like to imagine that we are rather more stable in our identities than impressionable puppies. But the truth is that we are more like the Westie and the elkhound than we think. Our sense of self and the views and behaviors that support it are mutable, forged again and again in the crucible of the circumstances we encounter and the company we keep. The effects of this can be profound. For example, white American boys who grew up with Black neighbors in the 1940s are more likely to be registered as Democrat voters seven decades later.[1] And these early experiences influence us in other ways too. In the 1990s, for example, the US Department for Housing and Urban Development ran an experiment that proved the radical effects our neighborhoods have on our health and economic prospects. Motivated by the deep inequalities that play out between neighborhoods, the department selected 4,600 of the poorest families they worked with. These families were then assigned to one of three groups. The first group retained access to their existing public housing. In other words, nothing changed for them. The second group were given a housing voucher, enabling them to move with no strings attached. A third group were also given a voucher, but to redeem it they had to move to a neighborhood with a poverty rate below 10 percent. In other words, this last group had their choice constrained to prompt more people to move to a richer neighborhood. A decade later, the results of this publicly funded experiment were published.[2] The data showed that those who moved to a richer neighborhood had better physical and mental health than those who did not. It also showed enormous economic gains for young children in terms of their future earnings. Those who moved at a young age, for example, were on a trajectory to earn $302,000 more over their lifetime than they would have done had they stayed put. For children over thirteen at the time of moving, though, it was a different story. These children experienced no gain in earnings; if anything, the effect of the move may have backfired.

So why might something as simple as moving house, especially if it takes us away from those we know and love, be so powerful? It is perhaps because we are built to be highly sensitive to the behavior of those around us. We are masterful observers, picking up on the subtlest of cues about what others around us think, feel, and do. Being able to assimilate by also endorsing these viewpoints is highly advantageous as being part of the herd ensures a level of social protection that benefits us greatly: we seek closeness wherever possible, allying ourselves to those we identify with even at the cost of our individuality. Because of this, we modify our actions to mirror the norms we pick up on, reinforcing them in the process. If this sounds dubious, consider that simply giving people information about what others do makes it much more likely that they will act in the same way, even when they had not done so previously. For example, telling those who have not yet paid their taxes that most people have already done so gets them to pay faster than they would otherwise,[3] and telling someone that their neighbors use less electricity than them reduces their consumption.[4]

While norms around tax payment and energy consumption might remain invisible because of a different social rule—"don't bore people by talking about taxes"—all kinds of information about what the majority of people think, feel, and do remains hidden for much more complex social reasons. Take, for example, shifting attitudes toward gay marriage. Over time, individuals may change their view, or demographic changes might mean that those who strongly opposed gay marriage are outnumbered by those who feel indifferent or positive about it. This adds up to a change in attitude at a population level and, eventually, most people become supportive of gay marriage. Although this shift has taken place, it may not have been visible. This means that many individuals will imagine that their privately supportive view on the matter would be rejected, even punished, by others if it were made public. This phenomenon, whereby multiple individuals believe that they are in a minority when in fact most people around them would agree with their stance is known as *pluralistic ignorance*. When the misperception is corrected, these individuals update their behavior in line with the true norm, meaning change can happen quickly. Such corrections can come in the form of pure information, such as feedback that most other people expressed a view counter to the perceived norm in private. It might also be initiated because of highly visible people, such as celebrities or influential people in a community, sharing their views. Or it could come from society-wide events, such as court rulings. Indeed, in the case of the Supreme Court of the United States' 2015 ruling in favor of gay marriage, research shows that people immediately saw this as a sign that most other people were pro-gay marriage even if their own view didn't change.[5] This licenses people who had previously been quietly supportive to become more vocal. Most people don't come out in favor of gay rights as a matter of principle; they do it because they want to make it clear that they are part of the social majority. Social acceptance looms large in our decisionscapes, coloring our actions in all kinds of ways.

As we see in the case of gay rights, our desire to fit in with the crowd can change things for good. Other examples of positive social change through making norms more visible include reducing binge drinking among college students by ensuring people know that their peers don't think excessive alcohol consumption is fun,[6] and increasing female workforce participation in Saudi Arabia by showing that most Saudi men think women should be able to work.[7] But our need to maintain close bonds can also have negative consequences. For example, in our quest to secure the approval of those we want to stay socially close to, we might agree or follow along with the group even when it puts us at a disadvantage. One of the most striking examples of this that I have seen in my own work came when I was interviewing young mothers in Toxteth, one of the most deprived areas of the United Kingdom, where at the time over 60 percent of children lived in poverty. I would describe my style—although perhaps that word is overly generous—as very casual. I enjoy field research and interviewing immensely, in part because it often allows me to dress at my preferred level of comfort. In these interviews, though, I felt embarrassed. As I looked down at my chewed cuticles and worn tracksuit bottoms, I met woman after woman who was perfectly manicured and dressed. They weren't, of course, dressed up for me. Nor did they care that I looked as though I'd dressed in the dark. They were dressed up for each other, following an unspoken code that dictated the $1,000 stroller they had to buy, the designer boots they ought to wear, and the exact right amount of jewelry to have on. The effect was striking: a visible in-group, a group of young mothers with their immaculate children congregating around the Children's Centre, which provides adult numeracy and literacy classes along with childcare. If this sounds unremarkable, consider that most of these mothers were living on $10 a day or less. Even between them they would have had nothing like the wealth needed to amass a designer wardrobe, and yet somehow each of them was perfectly turned out in this unofficial uniform.

For those who design welfare policy—and for those who read the uncharitable accounts of welfare recipients in tabloid newspapers—this kind of showy lifestyle can be enraging, and it is easy to see why. One woman I met, whose child was wearing Hugo Boss, told me that he had permanent diaper rash because she couldn't afford to change him more than twice a day. Another told me that she didn't eat until around 3:00 p.m. each day, at which point she would have a couple of biscuits courtesy of one of the staff at the Children's Centre. This, she said, was the only way she could afford her children's meals and something for herself to keep the hunger at bay before bed. While we talked, her daughter played on the floor with the contents of her mother's expensive-looking handbag. In none of the interviews was I left with the impression that the women saw their spending on designer gear as shameful, wrongheaded, or irrational. Honestly, from the outside, it looked as though, by spending money on clothes and top-tier prams, these mothers were prioritizing everything but their children. But judgments like this presuppose something important: that money and monetary transactions are the only way in which families invest in their children and relationships. In fact, this is far from the case, especially in resource-strapped environments. In many cases the social investments we make are the things that have longer-lasting value. If we look at this conspicuous consumption as an act of social collaboration, a nod of endorsement and belonging to a wider social class or group, the behavior begins to make sense. Social security—not the kind provided by government stipends but the kind that means someone will look after your kids when you have a job interview, give you a sofa or floor to sleep on when your landlord evicts you, or keep your secrets when you need advice—is also a currency. And the less traditional wealth you have, the more valuable it becomes. So it is not that these women are thoughtlessly spending on appearance. What looks from the outside like a handbag is actually an investment in social capital.

For these mothers, and those in twenty-one other Children's Centres across the United Kingdom, the work done by my colleagues went on to harness the value of these strong social bonds. Many people who access classes at Children's Centres do not complete them. We wondered if making attendees accountable to one another, through using a buddy system, might help reduce dropouts. To test this, we divided the learners into three groups: a control group who experienced the normal service; a group who were paid an individual bonus for attending at least 80 percent of the classes; and a final group who were assigned a random "buddy" from the class. In this final group, the bonus was paid out only if both buddies attended 80 percent of classes. The bonus worked as a motivator whatever the conditions attached to it, but it was much more effective for those students paired up with a buddy. On average, students with a buddy attended 75 percent of their classes compared to just 43 percent for those who were not given any additional incentive and 65 percent for those who were offered a bonus based only on their own attendance.

The Toxteth mothers helped me to understand another aspect of social belonging: being able to transgress is a privilege. In other words, a close social bond is a relatively more valuable currency when other aspects of your survival are precarious. Rich people can dress eccentrically, give their children unusual names, move to faraway locations, and reject the company of those they don't like because they have the luxury of money to solve their problems. Rich people enjoy doing these things. Why would they not? Being able to walk your own path opens all kinds of possibilities for self-actualization that conformity does not. Money enables us, in other words, to live our "one wild and precious life."[8] This prizing of individuality signals wealth in exactly the same way that expensive identikit apparel signals belonging in Toxteth. This is not a concept that occurs to most of us intuitively. More than this, research shows that those in positions of relative affluence generally assume that poorer people simply do not have the same drive to scratch the itch of these higher-level psychological needs. It is as if when they try to imagine the decisionscape of someone less well-off they drain the color, remove many of the objects, and generally think of a less rich canvas.

Work by Juliana Schroeder and Nicholas Epley, for example, shows that even when people are trying to help, they make the mistake of demeaning the needs of those they are helping.[9] For example, donors to a homelessness charity consistently underestimated the psychological needs of those who are homeless, assuming they only cared about solving the challenges faced by a lack of material resource. Minimizing or denying the human urge to meet needs such as living a meaningful life or having autonomy over our choices can lead to poor policy design and inefficient allocation of resources. This is more likely to be true when the social gap between those designing policy and those intended to benefit is larger. In Britain, for example, a top civil servant is five times more likely to have gone to a fee-paying school than the average person.[10] If you don't know what it is to have your choices constrained by poverty, you cannot easily understand the actions of those who do. This means that functional governments must concede that social progress is not something that can be done "to" or "for" people using traditional tools of policy alone. Governments can provide the resource, but social change must also be enacted "by" people, something that can only happen if those who hold power in communities use it to accelerate progress.

Does this sound fluffy? Naive? Hopelessly ideological? I'd think so were it not for the fact that some of the best work in social science has proven that tapping into the power dynamics of existing networks and getting those who hold power to initiate social change is possible. Take, for example, one of the most socially challenging environments around: middle school. Middle schools are crucibles of puberty. Most kids there are not having the time of their life; they're coming to grips with managing a new body and its weird needs, they're trying to look the way society tells them they should, and they're desperate to just fit in. The average middle schooler likely knows kids that are bullied and feels bad for them, but there is no way they are willing to do anything about it. But not all middle-school kids are average, and, like every social environment, some kids wield disproportionate influence. It was these kids—the ones who had enough social capital built up to successfully transgress the norms of turning a blind eye to bullying—that interested Betsy Levy-Paluck at Princeton University and her colleagues Hana Shepherd from Rutgers University and Peter Aronow from Yale University.[11] If we could just use the social status of these influential kids for good, they wondered, could we reduce bullying? The first task was to identify these kids. It's not like peer-led anti-bullying initiatives are new. In the TV series *Glee*, there is a whole storyline about the Bully Whips, a group of kids from the glee club assigned to tackle bullying by the principal. While the Bully Whips are a caricature, there is a lot of truth in the bit. When teachers choose ambassadors, they pick the "good" kids. They don't tend to think about who is likely to actually have sway with their peers, and if they do, the chances of them predicting this correctly are slim. Another way to identify kids with influence is to just pick the popular kids. Anyone who has ever been to school will know this is an easy task, but the problem is that these kids might be the bullies. What is really needed for a successful anti-bullying agenda is a list of kids who are liked and respected, qualities that may be a little harder to pinpoint without help. So Paluck and her colleagues had to figure out a way to recruit the right kids into their camp. To do this, they asked a simple question: Which ten kids at your school would you choose to spend time with if you could? This question went out to 24,191 middle schoolers across the 56 participating schools. For each school, the research team was then able to cross-reference the answers to figure out which kids were most popular among their peers. Interestingly, the kids that emerged through this process had a couple of characteristics that set them apart. Specifically, they were more likely to have an older sibling, to be dating someone in school, and to live in a house other kids admired. In other words, they were more socially mature and generally came from wealthier families.

Once they knew who these influential kids were, the team had to get them to intervene when it came to bullying. The existing anti-bullying curriculum was designed by adults, a sure-fire way to generate disengagement among teenagers. The new initiative, called Roots to reflect its grassroots generation, was designed by the kids. Only the objectives and framework for generating ideas were set by the adults. The kids designed several campaigns both online and in the schools. One involved giving out orange plastic wristbands to kids who were seen intervening in bullying incidents that said "A Roots student caught you doing something great." Because the wristbands, as well as the kids giving them out, were cool, everyone wanted one. Last, the research team had to measure the results. They chose a metric that gives a decent proxy for both how much bullying is going on and how much of a paperwork headache it is giving schools: disciplinary reports. When a bullying incident is observed and reported, it generates admin. Each report takes up to an hour to address and resolve. At the end of the yearlong study, schools that took part had a 30 percent reduction in these reports compared to those that did not participate.

Just as the bullies magically melted into nice kids, we are often completely unaware of the mental contortions we make to protect our social identities. Take, for example, the responses of unwitting experiment participants who were asked if holding migrant children in overcrowded cells at the US border is a human rights issue.[12] Democrats agreed 63 percent of the time if they were told President Obama initiated the policy and 95 percent of the time if they were told it was originated by President Trump. For Republicans, the direction flips: just 13 percent agree this is a human rights violation if told it was a Trump policy but 44 percent find it problematic under Obama. The partisan lines along which this experiment is divided show something helpful: there are clearly different baseline beliefs within a population (in this case, Republicans are much less likely to condemn harsh immigration controls than Democrats), but these positions are highly malleable depending on whether we believe them to have been endorsed by "our side."

We all arrange the objects in our decisionscapes differently. This is reflective of our personal tastes, preferences, and values. There is nothing wrong with this: each of us is entitled, so long as it is not breaking the law or endangering others, to live our lives according to our own priorities. What is a problem for us, though, is that external influences can cause parts of our decisionscapes to distort. Things that should remain in the background blow up, perhaps because they induce an emotional response in us. The things in our foreground get crushed or shunted backward by unwelcome distractions and demands on our attention. To make decisions that align with what we really want and value, we need to be alive to these distortions. The next chapter explores this phenomenon in more detail.

10 WHISTLE A HAPPY TUNE

Whenever I feel afraid
I hold my head erect
And whistle a happy tune
So no one will suspect I'm afraid
While shivering in my shoes
I strike a careless pose
And whistle a happy tune
And no one ever knows I'm afraid
The result of this deception
Is very strange to tell
For when I fool the people
I fear I fool myself as well
—*The King and I*, Richard Rodgers and Oscar Hammerstein (1951)

When I was fourteen, I took a Grade 3 singing exam. For those unfamiliar with the United Kingdom's musical grading system, you only need to know that this is not very impressive. While preparing for the exam, I experienced a pretty serious problem: when I practiced at home or with my teacher I was fine, but the moment I had to sing in front of anyone else, my voice climbed up into the back of my throat and wheezed out at least an octave higher than I intended. It wasn't just my voice: my heart thumped like a broken metronome, my vision tunneled, and my ink-stained palms began to sweat. When it came to sight reading, the score danced in front of my eyes, and even if I had been competent enough to tell what I was supposed to do, my ability to do it would have been close to zero. My music teacher, Mrs. Riley, came up with an idea. In her experience, nerves melted after the first few minutes. If you could get through the start of an exam, she said, you could get to the end of it. To help me survive this crucial period, she changed my opening number to "I Whistle a Happy Tune" from *The King and I*. It is a song about being nervous. If I looked or sounded like I was panicking, she reasoned, we could pretend I was acting the part. This turned out to be a pretty clever strategy. I kept it together just enough to scrape a pass in my exam. Years later, when I learned that the physiology of anxiety is extremely similar to the physiology of excitement, I thought back on the lyrics of that song—"The result of this deception/ Is very strange to tell/ For when I fool the people/ I fear I fool myself as well"—and wondered if there might have been more at play in that exam room than I had realized.

It turns out I was well behind the curve on wondering about how nerves and excitement could be interchanged to improve performance when it comes to singing, but the question led me to one of my favorite experiments of all time. In this study, Alison Wood Brooks from Harvard University invited some undergraduates to sing the first verse of "Don't Stop Believin'" by Journey in front of an experimenter.[1] In addition to a flat $5 payment for showing up, the participants were told that they could earn up to $5 in performance-based pay depending on the accuracy of their singing. Before completing the singing task, some participants were assigned to say a short statement, which either read "I am excited" or "I am anxious." The idea was that those who said they were excited would do better because they had reframed their nerves as excitement. The results supported the hypothesis: those who said they were excited performed best, while those who said they were anxious scored worst. This singing experiment hammers home that both our physiological response—sweaty palms, a racing heart, butterflies in the stomach—and our interpretation of it influence our ability to perform. It doesn't matter how rationally we think about the situation. The emotional response parks itself squarely in the foreground of our decisionscape and blots out everything else.

This is hardly news to the average human. But, in economics at least, it isn't how classic models of decision-making were typically constructed. Until fairly recently, we were imagined as coolheaded computational beings who factored a range of inputs into our decision. While the emotional consequences of a decision—for example, the fact we might regret a course of action if it didn't go as planned—could be weighed in, they were treated as anticipated. In other words, we would imagine those emotions as part of the bundle of costs or benefits associated with a particular outcome, but we would not experience the emotions unless that outcome came to fruition. However, we now know that *anticipatory* emotions play a significant role in decision-making.[2] We feel the painful effect of regret preemptively, for example, rather than simply thinking about it.

These flashes of anticipatory emotions precede the cognitive element of decision-making: our cool head comes preheated and, whether we like it or not, emotion distorts our judgment. Unlikely outcomes that should remain at a hypothetical distance are catapulted into the foreground.

The lightning speed of our emotional responses is an example of something Daniel Kahneman describes as "System 1" thinking in his book *Thinking, Fast and Slow*.[3] In contrast to System 2, our deliberative and dispassionate way of thinking, System 1 is fast and intuitive. System 1 exists to spare us effort. It does not require conscious thought and processes stimuli using simple rules of thumb. One such rule might be, for example, if I experience an emotional reaction then I should be led by that. System 1 also has a kind of master rule of thumb: if System 1 can handle it, don't bother System 2. In general, this is a smart way to manage the necessary trade-off between speed and rigor of thought in our daily lives. But it also means we can oversimplify or fall prey to mind tricks. This is perhaps easiest understood by looking at a sensory example of System 1 in action. Think back to the Ponzo illusion from the introduction (figure 10.1).

We can independently verify the fact that the two black lines are the same length and width, and yet the line at the top of the frame looks far bigger. Just as we cannot override the Ponzo illusion, we cannot turn off System 1, even when it is obviously misleading us, and emotionally fraught events put us at higher risk. Take the game blackjack, for example. For the unfamiliar, blackjack is a casino favorite where you must try and score as close to 21 as possible by turning over cards dealt to you and adding the number shown to the running total. For

Figure 10.1
Railway track with the Ponzo illusion overlaid.

example, if your first two cards are the three of clubs and the nine of diamonds, you have 12: 3 + 9. You then decide whether to turn over another card to go higher, an act that is informed partly by your current count and partly by the value of the dealer's single card. If you go over 21, you lose immediately. Each game is played against the house (the dealer): if the house scores closer to 21, it wins. If a player scores closer to 21, they win. Simple. So simple, in fact, that most regular blackjack players have memorized the optimal strategy for each combination of cards they might be served considering the dealer's card. The aim here is to play the numbers: if probability says you should stick, you stick. If it says you should take another card, you take another card. These probability tables are especially useful for helping guide the toughest calls. Every amateur player, for example, knows that if the dealer's card value is 7 or higher, then you should ask for another card if you have 16. The odds of winning at this point are slim, and the most likely outcome is that you will go bust. But on balance the best move you can make is to play on. When players find themselves in this situation, though, they often stick despite knowing it's the wrong move. Why? Because they feel the sting of regret in anticipation of their next move, putting them into a heightened emotional state that causes them to balk.[4] As a result, they increase their risk of losing the game but in a way that will feel more distant: by giving the house a chance to draw a better card. This is reminiscent of the Trolley Problem in chapter 3. Asking for another card is like pushing the man from the bridge: you cannot absolve yourself of the bad consequences in the same way you can if you do nothing.

The probabilistic approach of blackjack also goes against our natural tendency to want to minimize uncertainty. In any decision, there are several different ways a situation could turn out. Some have very high probabilities; some have very low probabilities. It is entirely rational to think through these various outcomes and to weigh up the impact of that outcome against the likelihood of it happening. However, when we make judgments and decisions in practice, we often overweight the first half of the equation, focusing largely on impact with little heed for probability. This is partly because we find uncertainty deeply uncomfortable. In its extreme, *intolerance of uncertainty*—a clinical term used to describe individual ability to tolerate conditions in which they have insufficient information—is a strong predictor of a range of anxiety disorders. People with health anxiety, for example, might experience a headache, wonder if it could be a sign of a serious condition, and then be unable to stop worrying until they get resolution of this uncertainty.[5] This can lead to expensive and unnecessary medical testing or obsessive reassurance-seeking (reassurance that is immediately punctured by the next unexplained bodily sensation).

While health anxiety requires psychotherapeutic treatment, most people have some level of aversion to uncertainty that—although it doesn't reach a clinical threshold—does influence their day-to-day decisions. Former professional poker player and behavioral researcher Annie Duke is successful exactly because she takes the card table mentality and holds it steady in the face of uncertainty. Her observation is that when we have less information than we would like to inform a decision, we often act as if we have no information at all.[6] For example, at work if someone asks you how long a task will take or how much something is likely to cost, you might answer that it's impossible to say or something similar. This is not true. It's very difficult to give a perfect estimate, but you can almost always give a ballpark or a range within which you are confident the answer will fall. Even a wide range is more helpful than no estimate at all. Duke describes this approach in terms of an *archer's mindset.* Waiting for perfect information is, in her opinion, like not shooting the arrow in an archery tournament for fear you won't hit the bull's-eye. Most of the time, her reasoning goes, your better bet is to shoot and at least hit the target. This advice is helpful in two ways. First, it lowers the burden of perfection by prizing a good fast shot over a delayed but perfect shot. Second, it endorses action.

Intolerance of uncertainty isn't the whole story, though. Some low-probability events are especially easy to recall, causing them to dominate more of our attention than they rationally ought to. Usually things that are distant, such as low-probability events, are abstract, hard to imagine in any level of detail, and operate at a high construal level. But certain kinds of low-probability events are overrepresented in the public consciousness, often because they are so extreme or rare that they become emotionally gripping public interest stories. This creates a mental reference library where these outcomes can be brought to mind far more readily and far more concretely than they should be. For example, it is easy to recall stories of people winning the lottery, but no one profiles those millions who faithfully buy a ticket each week and never win. There are many examples of how this *availability bias* can manipulate hypothetical distance with real-world consequences.[7] For example, in the year following the events of September 11, 2001, car accidents increased in the United States. Excluding the terrorists, 246 people died on the four planes that were hijacked. The events were so salient in the minds of the average American that many people chose to avoid flying, opting instead to drive cross-country when they needed to travel. By comparing road accidents before and after 9/11, researchers estimated that these emotionally driven decisions led to as many as 2,300 fatalities on the road after the attacks.[8] In other words, more than nine times as many people that died in the planes were killed on the road because the tiny probability of a repeat attack was blown out of all proportion by fear.

Availability bias like this can also galvanize positive action. In the United Kingdom, the heavy coverage of the illness and death of Jade Goody—a *Big Brother* contestant—from cervical cancer led to an increase in cervical smears and in disease diagnosis in women who had previously missed their appointments.[9] Availability bias can even sway government spending. In the 1990s, for example, the UK media was gripped by the tragic death of Leah Betts, a teenager who died after taking MDMA on a night out. In the years that followed there was huge investment, including from government, in anti-drug campaigns, many of which directly referenced Leah. There was no uptick, though, in alcohol-related campaigning even though, in 1995 alone, several thousand alcohol-related deaths were reported compared to just seventeen from MDMA.[10]

So how can we overcome, or even exploit, the siren song of emotional response when it is almost impossible to override? Many strategies echo some of the things I have already discussed in this book, such as perspective taking, asking someone else for their take, delaying the decision until a better moment, or finding ways to adopt a cool head. These are hard things to do in the moment but not impossible. In one set of experiments, participants were provoked into feeling anger or extreme frustration through abrasive interactions with the experimenter.[11] After the task, which involved solving problems while listening to music, some were instructed to "see the situation unfold through your own eyes as if it were happening to you all over again" while others were told to "move away from the situation to a point where you can now watch the event unfold from a distance . . . watch the situation unfold as if it were happening to the distant you all over again." A third group was given no specific instructions on how to reflect on what had happened. After the period of reflection, the researchers asked participants to describe their emotions through a short survey. Those who took the distanced fly-on-the-wall perspective were markedly less angry than those in the other two groups. This shows that it is possible to take advantage of imagined psychological distance in moments of emotional stimulation.

Of course, one obvious challenge here is that we need to be prompted to adopt a distanced perspective in the right moment. Sometimes this can be baked in by design. Research by Shayna Skakoon-Sparling and colleagues, for example, shows that sexual arousal leads to an increase in tolerance for risky sexual behavior, for example, an increased willingness to have sex with a new partner without protection.[12] With this in mind, making sure that the course of action most people would choose in a "cold," or unaroused, state is easy to take in a "hot," aroused, state can make a big difference to people's choices, especially regrettable ones. Many hotels in China, for example, have free condoms—often provided by local public health officials—right there on the nightstand. This is a smart design choice to help people avoid unprotected sex when they don't want to risk pregnancy or a sexually transmitted infection: the self-control needed to reach for the nightstand is far lower than the level needed to go to a shop or vending machine. By identifying and planning ahead for these predictable moments of low self-control, we can all neutralize the unhelpful distancing in our decisionscapes. For example, if I know I always end up buying chocolate on the train home, I can give myself another option by packing something healthy and delicious—a bag of nuts, perhaps—to munch on.

So far, most examples I have used show the lack of distance associated with emotional stimuli to be bad. But we may also be able to use emotional evocation for good. One neat example of this that has stuck in my mind longer than it perhaps should was a hack developed by an Uber driver I took a ride with. He had found that he was driving for too long, not taking enough breaks, and getting so tired he would make basic mistakes on the road. To remind himself to stop working and go home, he attached his child's first shoes to his dashboard.

"If I'm thinking about doing one more airport trip when I shouldn't, I see those and think 'Nah, I need to make sure I get home tonight.'" The slow creep of tiredness is hard to notice, but the sharp emotional jerk of seeing a sentimental item—at least for him—was enough to force him to reflect on whether it was time to go home.

In this section I have explored how our starting point matters when it comes to perspective. Each of us has a unique viewpoint, shaped by our circumstances, dispositions, cultures, and states of mind. This viewpoint acts like a lens on the decisionscape so that what I see and what you see will never look quite the same. By recognizing, experimenting with, and expanding these viewpoints, we can interrogate our decisions more robustly, giving ourselves the opportunity to make better choices.

Part III zooms way out from the bounds of the self to look at the bigger picture, the patterns that shape it, and how we come together to create something different from the sum of our parts.

III COMPOSITION

Art is the imposing of a pattern on experience, and our
aesthetic enjoyment is recognition of the pattern.
—Alfred North Whitehead[1]

11   THE BULL IN THE SKY

For thousands of years we have been talking about the bull in the sky.

It started with painting. Fifteen thousand years ago, some Mesolithic stargazer overlaid dots on one of the bulls at the caves in Lascaux, documenting a rudimentary constellation. In 2100 BCE, once we had gotten the hang of writing, the celestial bull popped up again, this time in the clay-set cuneiform tablets of *The Epic of Gilgamesh*. A couple of millennia later, the Egyptians carved the bull into the Dendera Zodiac while next door, in Canaan, the bull gave its name to the first letter of the Hebrew alphabet: aleph. And in Greek mythology Zeus presented himself as a heavenly bull to impress the Phoenician princess Europa.

While it could be possible that a single line of knowledge was transmitted from the cave painters of Lascaux through the ages, it is hardly likely. Instead, people independently looked at the night sky and saw "the bull" we know today as Taurus. But how does this happen? The heavens are not deliberately arranged in the shapes we see in the eighty-eight officially recognized constellations of the present day. The bull tells us nothing of the sky, but it does tell us something about the human brain.

In 2020, a high school junior named Sophia David latched on to this question: Why is it that we have seen the same shapes in random clusters of stars across time and cultures? Her hypothesis was that the answer lay in the mechanics of human vision. When I was Sophia David's age, I spent my summer traipsing around shopping centers, putting bubble bath in public fountains, and playing Nintendo 64. David, on the other hand, pursued her intellectual interest and contacted Danielle Bassett, a professor of physics, astronomy, and bioengineering at the University of Pennsylvania. Her idea, it turned out, was good, and she was invited to formally undertake her research at Professor Bassett's Complex Systems Lab.[1]

David and her research team built a model based on a simple simulation of how human vision takes in the night sky. The model replicates movements known as saccades—predictable jumps made by both eyes as they scan for information. This model was then combined with a map of the stars as they appear from earth, including data on how bright each star would look as well as its relative location. Using these three factors—how close the stars appear to one another, how bright they seem, and how our eyes take in information—the computer was able to reproduce many of the patterns that make up the official constellations. In other words, we see the bull so consistently because our eyes pick out patterns in predictable ways. It is as though our decisionscapes come preloaded with a basic set of templates that we seek to match the world to.

Sophia David's work builds on a large body of research into pattern recognition. Back at the start of the twentieth century, a movement known as Gestalt psychology emerged in Austria and Germany. The Gestalt psychologists put forward the idea that we perceive entire patterns rather than individual components and that the overall effect of the pattern can leave us with a different impression than merely taking in each of its separate elements. One of its founding figures, Kurt Koffka, asserted, "The whole is something else than the sum of its parts," a phrase frequently misquoted. In David's case, the "whole" is the constellation and the "parts" the individual stars. Her observation that we consistently see these same patterns evokes an old idea of the Gestalts known as the *principle of Prägnanz*. The principle of Prägnanz says that we impose order on the world by interpreting visual stimuli in the simplest way possible.

The Gestalts' research was foreshadowed in the art world. Claude Monet, for example, had been refining his Impressionist style for decades when the German psychologist Max Wertheimer introduced the principle of Prägnanz in 1923. Monet's work used fast brushstrokes and experimental color palettes to produce work that looks coherent and alive despite being choppy and blurred up close. In the words of Cher, the protagonist of the 1995 movie *Clueless*, "From far away, it's okay, but up close it's a big old mess." After Wertheimer and the Gestalts, the interplay between their work and art continued. Salvador Dalí, for example, made deep exploration of the "double image" in his work. In 1941, he painted a piece called *Bouche mystérieuse apparaissant sur le dos de ma nurse.*[2] The piece looks, at first glance, like the face of a woman. When you look more closely, though, you see that the "face" is in fact made up of pieces of a different picture entirely: a coastal scene in which a woman and a boy look out over the water. The "lips" and "nose" we see in the first impression are, in fact, the shawl and hat of a woman—Dalí's childhood nurse, as it turns out—while the eyes are a cluster of distant buildings across the lake. Double images like this allowed Dalí and others to explore how the pieces of an artwork add up to the whole. By deliberately creating works where the detail and the big picture are incongruent, he was able to violate and question the basic assumptions of composition.

Practical applications also sprung from the Gestalts' work. Dazzle camouflage, for example, exploited the brain's preoccupation with patterns to hide ships in the First World War. Traditional camouflage isn't very effective at sea, as it is extremely difficult to disguise a boat in the open ocean. Dazzle camouflage took a completely different approach. War ships were painted in bright colors and block black and white. These blocks were jagged and deliberately misaligned, breaking up the solid form of the boat. This meant the ship could be easily seen, but because the patterns didn't match up in a way that made sense to a brain looking for continuity, it was more difficult to accurately estimate its speed and direction. This seemed to be effective. According to one U-boat captain, "The dark painted stripes on her after part made her stern appear her bow, and a broad cut of green paint amidships looks like a patch of water. The weather was bright and visibility good; this was the best camouflage I have ever seen."[3]

Despite its uncommon success in capturing the cultural imagination, Gestalt psychology fell out of fashion as the field became more insistent on coherent theory and empirical evidence, but some of its core questions and insights survived. In the 1970s, researcher David Navon set about to prove whether

```
LLL      MM
LLL      MM
LLL      MM
LLL      MM
LLLLLLL  MMMMM
LLLLLLL  MMMMM
```

Figure 11.1

Two examples of Navon figures.

we see the "whole" or the "parts" first. He designed a series of figures: large capital letters composed of smaller capital letters that were either congruent with the larger letter they produced or incongruent. For example, a large L shape made up of small letter L's is a congruent stimulus while a large L made up of small M's is not.

Using these "Navon figures" enabled him to test the order in which we take in information: global shape or local detail first?[4] Navon found two things that backed the hypothesis that we see the big picture first. First, participants asked to identify the global letter did so faster than those asked to identify the smaller letters making it up. Second, when participants asked to identify the smaller letters were faced with a global letter that was incongruent, they took longer to give their answer. The same was not true when the smaller component letters were incongruent but the focus was on reporting the large global letter. In other words, at least when it comes to Navon figures, we see the global first and process the detail second.

Since Navon's first experiments, his figures have become a staple of psychology experiments, generating a wealth of new insights. One such experiment shows that people who were primed to see the global patterns in a Navon task were better at estimating distances and drawing accurate maps of an area they had studied compared to those who were primed to see the local pieces of the Navon figures.[5] Another showed that those who were primed to focus on the global Navon letter were better at a face recognition exercise than those who completed an unrelated task directly before.[6] By contrast, those who were primed to look at the smaller letters within the figure were worse at face recognition than everyone else. An insight like this is useful, as facial recognition is both important and unreliable in high-stakes situations, such as suspect identification. One of the reasons it is unreliable is that the witness must translate their overall—global—interpretation of the suspect into specific—local—details about individual features. It seems that prompts to focus on the big picture can inoculate against the kinds of mistakes that creep in when we make this shift. This insight might help us in other situations where the psychologically proximal threatens to blot out everything else. It may feel weird to spend two minutes calling out the global letters shown in Navon figures before an identity parade or a strategy meeting, but it could just be worth it!

Around the time Navon was running his experiments, the aerospace industry was designing new products to help its pilots. It turns out it might have been valuable to compare notes, especially when it came to understanding how we allocate and switch attention between the detail and the big picture. In 1980, NASA published a technical paper assessing one of these innovations titled *Cognitive Issues in Head-Up Displays*.[7] The purpose of the work was to study whether the use of technology, in this case, displays that superimpose flight information over a pilot's field of vision, alters performance compared to the traditional approach of looking away to check the cockpit instrument panel during landing. It seems a reasonable hypothesis that the head-up displays would improve the pilot's performance. The more time the pilot can spend looking at the big picture—that is, the world beyond the window—the better. And head-up displays mean they never have to take their eyes off the route ahead. To test this, the researchers put several commercial airline pilots into a flight simulator. They ran a series of landing simulations varying conditions such as wind shear, turbulence, and visibility. In some of the simulations there was an unexpected object—another plane—blocking the runway. For each simulation they recorded data on pilot reaction times, actions taken, and whether the pilot was wearing a head-up display. In some cases, the displays did lead to better performance, but they failed in one critical way: when the pilots wore them, they took more than twice as long to notice the other plane blocking the runway, and two of the pilots failed to notice it entirely.

The pilots who didn't see the plane were experienced. One was a captain, whose performance had been exceptional on all other aspects of the task. The other was a first officer with 2,000 hours in this type of aircraft under his belt. So how was it that they failed to notice the plane? The answer is that they were experiencing a phenomenon known as *inattentional blindness*, a failure to notice an obvious but unexpected object when attention is engaged on another task. It isn't just pilots who are susceptible to this. In a similar study, fifty experienced surgeons performed a procedure on a cadaver as part of a training exercise.[8] Half the surgeons used a regular monitor as an aid, but half used a new augmented reality headset to help them navigate the procedure. Like the pilots, the augmented reality headset should have helped focus attention as it meant they never had to look away from the procedure. But, just as the pilots failed to see the plane on the runway, 60 percent of the surgeons wearing the headsets failed to spot a foreign object in the body. Without the headset, meanwhile, this happened just 32 percent of the time. In these cases of inattentional blindness, the error might result from incomplete switching of attention. Pilots and surgeons must alternate between looking at a separate set of displays and then looking at the flight path or surgical field. As they do this, they are also changing their level of attention. They must focus closely on the instruments but take in the wider visual field when looking at the job itself. This switching demands our eyes and brain to adjust between two different modes of operation. I say eyes and brain, but in this case, they are one and the same. The retinas are essentially two pieces of brain extruding from the cranial vault. The activity experienced by the retina, therefore, has a direct and large impact on the rest of the brain.[9] In other words, whatever is in our visual environment has a direct impact on our state of mind.

This isn't just about what we see. The visual system also sends signals to our brain about the appropriate level of vigilance. For example, when the light is low, our brains begin to wind down, sending instructions to our metabolic systems and other parts of the body to do the same. When we relax—just as we do when it gets darker—our pupils dilate. This allows us to take in more of the visual field, like some kind of panoramic mode has been turned on. Simply looking out at a vast open space is enough to trigger this response. When we look at open space, our gaze roams and naturally softens. When we look at something close up, like instruments in a cockpit, for example, the opposite happens. Our eyes converge, the aperture narrows, and we experience, although we may not perceive it, a tunneling of our vision. When the pilots have to physically look up and down between the instruments and the window, they automatically toggle between these two modes. This means they are physiologically geared up to take in the big picture when their head is up and the detail when their head is down. But when the instruments are superimposed over the visual field, they may end up in a kind of limbo, no longer switching their attention as effectively between the detail and the big picture. They might think they are taking in the wider panorama when they are, in fact, still focused on their instruments.

Beyond pilots and surgeons, examples of inattentional blindness abound. People preoccupied by their phones fail to notice money hanging from trees or unicycling clowns in the street.[10] More importantly, cops miss the presence of a firearm during inspections, eyewitnesses to a crime fail to notice anything unusual, and workers overly focused on technical tasks miss the signs that could prevent fatal construction accidents.[11] If you've seen the "invisible gorilla" video, you have likely experienced inattentional blindness for yourself. In the video, viewers are instructed to count the number of times the team dressed in white passes the ball to one another. They then watch a short film in which the team, swarmed by opponents wearing black, pass a ball back and forth. At the end, the viewers are asked for the number of passes, but they are also asked whether they saw anything unusual. In the original experiments, 58 percent say no. The other 42 percent, on the other hand, are aghast.[12] How, they wonder, did most people fail to notice the large gorilla walking across the frame? Most of us are not used to counting basketball passes, so perhaps our inability to spot changes in the scene is only a result of our naive overfocus.

To test whether this was the case, a group of researchers conducted an even more ridiculous version of the invisible gorilla experiment.[13] This time, they wanted to see whether a group of highly trained experts would fail to spot the gorilla in a task they performed daily. To do this, they asked twenty-four radiologists to review a series of lung scans with the goal of finding lung nodules. The last scan included a picture of a gorilla forty-eight times the size of the average lung nodule. When asked if they saw anything unusual beyond the nodules, just four of the twenty-four radiologists reported noticing the gorilla. The others had no clue. Interestingly, the study also included an eye-tracking component. This revealed that most of the radiologists who missed the gorilla looked directly at it while reviewing the scan.

This reliance on patterns, expectation, and prediction is not limited to visual perception. In another experiment, researchers asked their participants to try and remember a list of words and then tested their recall.[14] The words are all connected: for example, bed, rest, awake, yawn, blanket, snooze, drowsy. However, the thing that connects them (in this case "sleep") is missing. The researchers found that between 40 and 55 percent of people falsely recall having seen the missing word. In some ways, this is the opposite of the issue experienced by surgeons and pilots: they fail to see something right in front of their eyes while those experiencing false recall think they have seen something that wasn't there. But the two phenomena are linked. In both cases, our brains fill in the blanks with what they expect to see because they are unable to attend to all of the details. With the pilots, this is because the information on the display dilutes attention, causing their brains to fill in the surrounding scene with a projection of what is most likely to be going on. With the falsely recalled word, it is because there is too much detail for our brains to recall it all with accuracy and so—just as the principle of Prägnanz might predict—we make things easier by identifying the broader lexical pattern as the reference point. In both cases, this effortless confabulation leads us to make a mistake. It is as though our decisionscapes begin from the point of what we expected to see and are then updated as we get new information.

Our propensity to see patterns is so powerful we barely even notice it. Most of us can, for example, hear a piece of familiar music in a completely new key and find that we have no trouble at all anticipating the next note. This sensitivity to patterns can lead us to the borders of irrationality, though. Casinos are full of people who think they have "a hot hand" or, conversely, that their losing streak must mean they're due a payout soon. Conspiracy theories, too, show how seductive the promise of a pattern can be. In a 2021 survey, for example, the research company PRRI found that—in a nationally representative sample of around 5,000 adults—15 percent of Americans agreed with the statement "the government, media, and financial worlds in the U.S. are controlled by a group of Satan-worshipping pedophiles who run a global child sex trafficking operation."[15] Of course, there is likely some nontrivial portion of respondents who just think it's fun to agree with something so outlandish, but 15 percent is enough to suggest that the core of the QAnon conspiracy theory has made its way out of the bowels of the internet and into mainstream society.

We even end up drawn to patterns when we are trying to act in a way that is random. Mathematician Alex Bellos found that seven is the most common answer when people are asked to choose their favorite number.[16] It is also overrepresented when people are asked for a *random* number between one and ten, a fact exploited by those who design certain carnival games. In fact, our capacity for randomness when it comes to number generation is very minimal.[17] Poker players know this and find ways to outsource randomness. They might, for example, set a rule that they will fold if the second hand on the clock on the wall is past the one o'clock mark and play on if it is between twelve and one o'clock. While poker players are deliberate, without explicitly understanding our inability to act randomly, we have at various points in history developed survival strategies that use randomization to make us less predictable. In his book *The Secret of Our Success*, Joseph Henrich describes the practice of "pyro-scapulimancy"—burning the shoulder bones of animals to decide where to hunt.[18] The bones are typically stripped and dried before being burned over a fire. As the bones heat up and burn, cracks appear. There are so many factors that determine where the first crack appears that it is essentially random, but the crack is taken as a divine signal of where to hunt. Henrich suggests that, by following the direction indicated by the first cracks in the burning bones, those who practice pyro-scapulimancy are increasing their chances of a successful hunt by exploiting the merits of randomness. Humans, and our penchant for predictable patterns, are easy to avoid if you're a savvy caribou. But randomness is impossible to dodge day after day, and so hunting techniques that find ways to exploit it will be more effective over a sustained period.

This eye for patterns makes sense when we think about the evolutionary advantages it bestows. Our survival is tightly tied to our ability to make predictions about what is likely to happen next based on what we have observed in the past. The seasons follow a set pattern, we need to know the routines of animals to be able to hunt them, and resources tend to clump together in ways that might reveal where we can find water, for example. Our propensity for pattern recognition refines as we gain experience of the world, but, in some cases, we might actually be more adept at very young ages. For example, in one study children between one a half years old and two and a half years old were shown how to activate a machine that played music by placing two similar bricks on top of it.[19] They were also shown that the machine did not play music if two different bricks were used. When given the chance to try and activate the machine themselves, the toddlers were good at the task, frequently choosing two similar bricks and successfully activating the machine. When children aged three—just six months older—were given the same task, they performed no better than chance, choosing pairs of similar and different bricks at an equal rate. The researchers were able to demonstrate that this is because they were, by age three, paying more attention to the individual objects, thereby losing focus on the relationship between them.

So it is clear that patterns have a huge sway on how we interpret information, but, as we will see in the next chapters, many of the most influential patterns are human constructions, designed to help us make sense of the world.

12   ROBBING THE RECORD STORE

It's 2001. Your favorite band has just released a new album and you can't wait to hear it. You wake up early and head to your local record store. You walk to the rock aisle, find your band's little section, and flick through the CDs until you find it. You sneak a quick look over your shoulder. The store assistants are busy getting set up for the day, so no one notices you slip the plastic case into one of the many pockets of your cargo pants and walk out.

I would imagine most readers do not think this is acceptable behavior. However, imagine instead that rather than going to the record store, our antihero is on his computer. He loads up Napster (2001's go-to peer-to-peer file sharing platform) and downloads the same album free of charge. Suddenly his actions seem a little more relatable; if you have not pirated music yourself, you almost certainly know people who have. After all, in 2018 38 percent of music consumers were still engaged in some kind of music piracy, despite the ubiquity of free (and perfectly legal) streaming services.[1] Consider that the United Kingdom's Intellectual Property Office recently confirmed that sharing passwords for services such as Netflix is a crime, and perhaps it's a little clearer how these acts are so ubiquitous.[2]

So what is going on here? Why does the physical crime feel so much worse than its virtual counterpart?

In part, it is because the act of illegally downloading music does not fit our perception of what a theft looks like. When we walk out of a store without paying, we recognize that we are stealing and, as such, we feel very strongly that our actions are somehow immoral and harmful. Behind the glow of the screen at home, though, the illicit nature of what we are doing feels distant and abstract. We don't see ourselves as lone criminals but instead as part of a large community of people all sharing and enjoying music. This mindset also explains how some white-collar crime happens. Insider trading, for instance, doesn't *feel* like a crime: a friend gives you a tip, you buy some stock, the value goes up, you cash out. You didn't steal the stock from someone else; you paid the fair market value for it at the time of purchase. You didn't put the company in jeopardy. In fact, you gave it a vote of confidence by putting your money behind it. And that friend who gave you the tip? They made you feel like a trusted confidant. The victims are ghosts in a counterfactual universe in which you didn't buy the stock; your actions caused them not to exist. When you consider all of this, the overall sense is that you've been part of a secret and exciting adventure, not a damaging crime. We have seen echoes of this in several previous chapters. For example, pushing the man from the bridge fits the mental model for murder, but pulling the lever to reroute the trolley does not. Similarly, protecting your stressed-out colleagues feels like the kind of thing a good person would do, so much so that it masks the fact you are acting against the interests of the children you are trying to place in foster homes.

One way to combat this issue of not fitting the archetypal image of a crime is to try and change the mental model people hold. Over the years many campaigns have taken this approach. For example, in the early 2000s an advertising campaign directed at the new but alarmingly rife phenomenon of digital piracy ran in cinemas around the world. The ads showed a man stealing various objects before equating these obvious acts of theft to illegally acquiring and sharing movies. The line "You wouldn't steal a car" clearly resonated, although perhaps not as the creators had hoped. The campaign was widely ridiculed, with spoof versions of the ad and memes being produced for years after. It may even have led to *more* theft by giving the impression piracy is the norm.[3] But part of the idea behind the ads was actually pretty good. Creating a new, easily recognizable example of a behavior or situation can make it easier for us to correctly identify it when we see it. It is like installing an upgrade to the templates we each draw on to structure our decisionscapes.

This was part of the motivation behind a campaign in Tanzania aimed at reducing the prevalence of relationships between predatory older men and young girls.[4] Such relationships put girls at higher risk of contracting HIV and are often exploitative in other ways too. The researchers behind the campaign figured that if they could increase community intervention, then they would reduce the number of men successfully preying on younger girls. But increasing intervention is hard: you need bystanders to know what they are looking for, to reject the behavior as a norm, and to know what to do when they see it.

The solution was the creation of a multimedia campaign that featured stories about "Fataki," an older male character whose gross attempts to seduce younger women were repeatedly foiled by bystander intervention. The goal was to give people a word—Fataki—and a prototype to help them more readily identify inappropriate behavior as well as to model effective ways to intervene. It worked: the more people were exposed to the campaign, the more they discussed the issue of cross-generational sex, and the more likely they were to intervene when they saw predators in action. Creating a new mental model and a language to discuss it helped bring an invisible issue into the public consciousness.

Of course, organic versions of this exact process happen all the time, and they can make the problem worse. For example, when it comes to sexual assault, at least in the United States, the concept of the serial rapist has strongly informed the design of assault prevention policies as well as our public understanding of what a predator looks like. In the serial rapist model, most rapes are committed by a small number of perpetrators who attack many different people and are inherently bad; finding and catching these individuals is therefore critical to solving the problem. While we wait for the cops to track down these comic book baddies—needles in a haystack of good people—we deploy a range of interventions that focus on making women less vulnerable to attacks. We dole out rape whistles, mace, and advice about how to make yourself less vulnerable. It is a neat narrative with simplistic solutions, but it is not founded. In fact, sexual assault is perpetrated by a much wider range of individuals, many of whom slowly begin to engage more in these behaviors over time as they find themselves in environments that license them.[5] By mischaracterizing the concept of a rapist in the public imagination, we make it much harder to spot inappropriate behavior before it escalates and to gain backing for policies that address the true root causes of the issue. Being deliberate about the way we cast specific issues, and the symbols, such as the Fataki, we create to represent them can go a long way.

Our responses to CD theft, the Fataki, and the myth of the serial rapist can all be explained by a phenomenon known as the *prototype effect*.[6] In psychology, a prototype is a mental representation that serves as a reference point when we think about a particular category. For example, if we think of cakes, we might have a prototypical cake—the cakeiest of all cake—in mind. The prototype cake might, for example, be large enough for a group of people to share, cylindrical, iced, and topped with berries and candles. Not all cakes will look exactly like this one, but the prototype will help us differentiate between a cake and a bun, for example. The most important or obvious features of the prototype are the ones that come to mind fastest when we think of the category. If something possesses the features of the prototype, we might take that as evidence it belongs in the category. Because these kinds of judgments are instantaneous, they can be wrong. For example, I am tall. When I have long hair, I am usually correctly identified as a woman. When I have short hair, though, I am routinely misgendered by people seeing the features of a prototype (prototypical men are tall and have short hair) without taking a closer look. Prototypes appeal to our affinity for patterns, but they are also made more or less effective as a result of psychological distance. The further my cake deviates from the prototype, be it in size, toppings, shape, or color, the harder your brain will have to work to classify it as a cake. We can manipulate this distance, bringing something closer to the prototypical ideal of the category as a result. For example, in one experiment, participants were presented with the details of a murder case that had been witnessed by a minor, a girl called Jessica Miller.[7] After seeing the details of the case, including information about the witness, they were shown one of two versions of a short statement from the defense attorney. Both statements were identical but for one small detail. The first stated, "I would like to draw your attention to one important circumstance regarding Jessica Miller. A child is less reliable as a witness. Therefore, Jessica Miller is less reliable as a witness." The second variant gave Jessica's age rather than referring to her using the prototypical language of "a child": "A twelve-year-old is less reliable as a witness." After reading the case details and the statement, the participants were asked to say how much they agreed with the assessment that Jessica Miller was an unreliable witness. Those who had been exposed to the generalization "a child is less reliable as a witness" were more likely to agree than those who had been told "a twelve-year-old" is unreliable. The underlying explanation for this finding is that, although everyone would agree Jessica Miller is a child, the prototypical child in most people's minds is younger than Jessica—maybe seven years old—and likely possesses more qualities associated with unreliable testimony than the average twelve-year-old might. When Jessica is described as a child, our perceptions of her drift toward the prototype, making her seem younger and less reliable than she would otherwise. The researchers ran the same tests varying Jessica's age from four years old to nineteen years old. When Jessica was very young, the prompt that included her specific age was more likely to make people doubt her reliability. This is because a four-year-old seems less reliable than the older child implied by the prototype. When she was older—nine, twelve, fourteen, seventeen—casting her as a child made the accusation of unreliability more persuasive. Again, the features that spring to mind when we imagine the prototype of a child are likely to be more strongly associated with a lack of reliability than when we imagine an older child. Older Jessica was made more babyish by the magnetic pull of the prototype.

The examples so far have operated on the assumption that people share an understanding of prototypes: that the template features of our decisionscapes are shared. That is, we understand the world to be carved into a common set of categories, and we tend to organize things into those categories in a concordant way. But sometimes our definitions don't line up, which can create problems of an entirely different nature.

13 I GUESS THAT'S WHY THEY CALL IT THE BLUES

It was during the gap between his terms as chancellor of the exchequer for the United Kingdom that William Ewart Gladstone decided to count how many times different colors were referenced in the works of Homer.[1] Across *The Iliad* and *The Odyssey*, he recorded 170 references to black, 100 to white, thirteen instances of red, and cameo appearances from yellow and green. Blue, though, never appeared. Gladstone was gripped by curiosity. Why was the Aegean Sea described as "wine dark" and the sky "bronze"? Was Homer color-blind? Did he see blue but lack the word to express it? Or is it, perhaps, only possible to notice a color once you have named it?

Gladstone was not the only one captured by this mystery. As others charted the development of color in other languages, they noticed a pattern. First come names for basic contrast—dark and light, black and white—then reds appear, followed by greens and yellows. Blue is typically added last.[2] What Gladstone was observing in Homer was a language of color still in development. The enigma of the Greek blue doesn't end there, though. Today, in modern Greek, the color space is still divided differently than in English. Specifically, Greek speakers split the blue color space into two distinct pieces: *ghalazio* (light blue) and *ble* (darker blue).[3] Differences like this can be seen between many languages around the world. The Berinmo language in Papua New Guinea, for example, lacks a distinction between green and blue, but differentiates between two colors in that region that the English language does not: *nol* and *wor*. In experiments with adult speakers of English and Berinmo, participants find it easier to discriminate between shades when their language places them on either side of a "category" border. For English speakers, for example, it is easy to identify differences between green and blue but very hard to discriminate between nol and wor, even when the gap between shades is equivalent in both cases.[4] This phenomenon is known as *categorical color perception*. By cutting the color wheel into slices and naming them—pink, yellow, brown—we open up perceptual distance at the boundaries that did not exist before. Colors, which feel so fundamental, are, at least in part, constructed by language (so much so that when Greek speakers learn to speak English and use Greek less they begin to "see" colors in a way that is more consistent with the English-speaking division of the color spectrum).[5] It isn't just colors. Even the way we divide up our bodies varies based on the language we speak.[6] For example, while in English "hand" and "arm" are considered different body parts, in many languages, the whole upper limb has a single name. These concepts can be difficult for us to internalize. Whether it's body parts or color palettes, we are so used to thinking in terms of the discrete categories that we are familiar with that we forget the lines between them are blurry and arbitrarily drawn.

This categorical thinking bleeds into every aspect of our lives. In the financial sphere, for example, because discrete dollars are considered as categories, consumers reliably judge the difference between $4.00 and $2.99 to be larger than that between $4.01 and $3.00, even though both are $1.01 apart.[7] In investing, where the stakes may be much higher, categories are a core feature of the market. For example, we might group options by things like asset class, industry, or risk level. Categories like this make it easier to navigate highly complex financial markets, but they also fool us into thinking options within the category are homogeneous. This can cause individuals issues when it comes to investing our money—we might double down on sectors we previously had success in, for instance, without paying attention to the unrelated factors that determined that previous success—but it might also cause problems for whole parts of the investment market that don't neatly fit into the existing categories. Take, for example, social investments. These kinds of investments promise a double payout: they're good for the investor's bottom line, and they also produce social good. Being able to evaluate prospects in terms of both kinds of outcome is essential to get the best out of the social investment market, but the existing categories of "for profit" and "for good" muddy our ability to do this. Research shows that this has a negative impact on the quality of investment decisions: when your choices are neither fish nor fowl you simply don't know what to make of them. To improve investment outcomes, Matthew Lee and his collaborators Arzi Adbi and Jasjit Singh tried a different approach: removing the labels that identified the options as a "for-profit company," "charity," or "social enterprise."[8] By making these categories invisible and less salient, they found that participants allocated their investments with a stronger focus on outcomes.

The power and risks of categorization also extend into our social interactions. For example, we treat people differently based on social categories we hold in mind and place them in. In one experiment on an online retail platform, researchers varied the skin color of a hand holding a product being sold. When asked, many—although of course not all—people would say, and truly believe, they would not treat a seller differently based on skin color, but this is not borne out in the experiment. When the product was held by a Black person's hand, the seller received 13 percent fewer responses and 17 percent fewer offers.[9] When they did receive an offer for the product, it was lower than if a white hand was featured in the picture. All this might suggest we should eschew categorization, but that would be as impossible as it is impractical. Our brains are evolved to take shortcuts that help us simplify and make sense of the complex information we encounter every day. Grouping things together based on similarities is a highly effective way to do this and so erasing or ignoring those categories is generally unhelpful. Despite this obvious fact, though, we frequently try to overwrite or ignore the mental categories we hold, often for good reason.

To demonstrate this, Evan Apfelbaum and his colleagues designed an experiment involving a version of the retro boardgame Guess Who?[10] In Guess Who? each of the two players chooses a "secret identity" card from the deck. This card assigns them one of twenty-four personas. The objective of the game is to correctly guess the identity of your opponent before they guess yours. The only available information about the identities is on the picture cards displayed on the board. These cards show the name and face of each of the twenty-four possible personae. To narrow down the options, the two players take it in turns to ask one another questions that can be answered yes or no. For example, "Is the character male?" or "Does she have red hair?" In the redesigned version of Guess Who? half the characters were white and half were Black. This means that asking about race is highly advantageous since it allows you to eliminate 50 percent of the identities in one go. The question was, would people deploy this tactic, or would they shy away from asking about race? When white players were paired with a white partner, they asked a question like "Is the person Black?" 57 percent of the time. When they were paired with a Black partner, though, they censored, only asking 21 percent of the time. When the researchers asked an independent group of reviewers to rate the questioners after the game, those who had avoided mentioning race were identified as being *more* biased than those who mentioned it. In other words, the deliberately color-blind strategy made people look more racist. To double-check that the participants were censoring, rather than simply spectacularly bad at Guess Who?, the researchers tested another version of the game. In this format, each persona card had a white or black dot in the bottom left corner of the picture. The dots were uncorrelated with the race of the person on the card and were also evenly distributed so that half were white and half black. In this version of the game, most people asked about the color of the dot. In other words, the omission is about social categories and not colors. In a separate set of experiments, the researchers had children play the game without the dots.[11] They wondered whether there is a typical age at which children gain enough experience to know that asking about race is considered socially taboo. If so, they reasoned, then children a little younger than this threshold age might actually be better at Guess Who? because they are not willing to sacrifice a smart play—asking about the race of the character—in order to seem socially polite. This is exactly what they found. Eight- and nine-year-olds were able to beat their ten- and eleven-year-old opponents because they asked about race. Their decisionscapes were unfiltered, giving them the edge.

Since categories are both useful and inescapable, what matters is that we understand the way these categories govern our perceptions and actions. In particular, when it comes to grouping people, the lines we draw in our definitions often serve the people who get to draw them by following and exaggerating existing differences in the world. For example, we might use a country border, the footprint of an empire, a language barrier, or a religious difference to help us decide where the cutoff lies between racial or ethnic groups. The resulting categories reflect and reinforce the order of things in our societies, becoming so strongly internalized over time that we think they are natural. In other words, the way we *talk* about people and ideas reflects the way they are viewed and treated in society, but it also changes it: language deals in psychological distance, amplifying social proximity within groups by highlighting a shared identity, and building distance between groups by inventing and naming a new point of difference.

To understand how this works in action, imagine you are a second-generation Lebanese immigrant living in the United

Kingdom. When you receive the census, you will be asked to identify your national identity and your ethnicity. Among the options given, you might choose "British" and "Arab" for your answers. Now imagine you have a cousin whose parents moved from Lebanon to the United States the same time yours moved to Britain. When your cousin answers the US census, he is asked about his race and origin, not his nationality and ethnicity. This requires him to check a box to select his race and to write his origin freehand. The options for race are limited, and under the "white" option, Lebanese is given as an example. Because of the way this paperwork is designed, people whose families come from all over the Middle East and North Africa end up being listed as white on the official record, even if they—or others—do not see themselves this way.[12] This may seem trivial, but it may not be. There is evidence suggesting, for example, that Americans with North African or Middle Eastern ancestry have a higher risk of diabetes than non-Arab, non-Hispanic, whites.[13] This increased risk might be because of genetic predisposition but could also be exacerbated by a lack of guidance relevant to members of these communities. With better data, public investments in screening and prevention could be targeted more effectively. Instead, though, the administrative lines, drawn by the census to carve people up, render Arab Americans and their needs invisible.

These past few chapters have explored the various ways in which our predilection for patterns influences our judgment and behavior. We see links where there may be none, and we fail to notice how the categories we create to simplify the world around us impose an invisible template on our decisionscapes. These templates are helpful because they are shared. They imbue us with a kind of collective intelligence by giving us a common shorthand and a guarantee that we are looking at the world in the same way. The next chapter explores this collective intelligence in more detail, examining the relationship between the individual and the crowd.

14   THE SUM OF OUR PARTS

In the summer of 2021, Finland's football team was set to make its debut in the UEFA European Championship finals. The first game of their tournament would be against fellow Scandinavians Denmark, a team Finland had last beaten in 1949. They would go on to break that losing streak and win this game, but no one would remember that. Instead, the match would go down in footballing history as the one where Danish midfielder Christian Eriksen died on the pitch.

Eriksen was on form. He had scored in the 2018 World Cup, played in the Euros before, and was on a run of twenty-five consecutive appearances for his country. In his own words, "I didn't see it coming at all." It was just before halftime when Eriksen had the cardiac arrest. Joakim Maehle took a throw-in for Denmark. Eriksen passed the ball back, and then he fell. It was immediately obvious from the way he went down that things were serious. The medical team came running onto the pitch and began efforts to revive him. The Danish players formed a protective ring around their teammate. And the Finnish fans, who moments earlier had considered Eriksen the enemy, donated their flags to help block him from the crowd and cameras. Eriksen was eventually brought back to life. As he left the pitch, he held his head up on the stretcher just enough for the cameras to show he was conscious. A stunned quiet fell on Parken Stadium. And then, from the low buzz of conversation, a call went up from the Finnish stands, "Christian!"

It hung for a moment and then, this time from the Danish stands, a response: "Eriksen!"

Back and forth they went: "Christian! Eriksen!" Louder and clearer with each round. Someone began punctuating the pause in between with a drumbeat. Fifteen thousand voices coming together with no obvious coordination to celebrate the midfielder as he was taken to hospital.

Most of us will recognize this sensation of being at one with a crowd. Dance floors, protests, and theater audiences all create eerie moments of synchronicity among many people. Over a hundred years ago, the sociologist Émile Durkheim dubbed the phenomenon *collective effervescence*.[1] For Durkheim, collective effervescence happened when a group of people simultaneously experienced the same thought or performed the same action. In such moments, the individuals involved manifest a kind of Gestalt spirit, creating something collective that is different from the sum of its parts.

There are examples, for instance, of crowds working to unite lost children with their parents by calling the name of the child in a kind of audible wave, fanning out from the epicenter and then, once their parent is located, guiding them in by relaying the call back down the line. Since Durkheim, there have been hundreds of studies on these phenomena of collective effervescence and action, examining cultural events and group dynamics around the world. This work reveals something surprising. When we come together in large groups, we don't just *feel* connected, we are connected on a deep physiological level. Somehow, we transcend our individual identities so that the crowd becomes like one larger being composed of thousands of individual lives. To understand how this works, Dimitris Xygalatas and his colleagues studied participants and spectators in a fire-walking ritual in Spain and found that the heart rates of individuals within the crowd began to synchronize as collective effervescence took hold, especially if those individuals were watching a relative walk through the fire.[2] This isn't just about the fact the event itself is exciting. Another of Xygalatas's studies, this time in collaboration with researchers from Brazil, the United Kingdom, and the United States, looks at the effects of watching live sport on spectators.[3] To do this, they hooked basketball fans up to a series of monitoring devices. The fans who watched the game on TV with a small group of people clearly enjoyed it; their heart rates went up when things got exciting, and they were highly invested in the action. But there was nothing synchronous about their physiological responses when compared to the others watching the game. The fans in the stadium, on the other hand, seemed to transform into one enormous organism. Their autonomic nervous systems started to fire as one, they reported a more "transformative" experience, and they identified more strongly with the group of fellow fans. The experiment showed that it wasn't just about the game, it was about the dynamic that unfolds between fans. It was as if, for a brief moment, their decisionscapes perfectly matched onto one another and they experienced the world in the same way.

This ability to operate at a level above our individual selves may have advantages for us collectively. At the most obvious level, the crowd provides protection since thousands of humans are a more difficult target than a small number of individuals. But crowds can also outperform individuals because they benefit from the aggregate abilities of many thousands of people. To take a very simple example, think of a crowd performing a song. In 2017, concertgoers in London's Hyde Park waiting to see the band Green Day began singing along to Queen's "Bohemian Rhapsody." Within a few seconds the sound of the crowd had overwhelmed the park speakers, meaning the music itself was almost inaudible. However, the crowd kept time and kept up the melody for the entire duration of the song. More than this, it sounded good. If you were to take any individual from the crowd at random and ask them to sing an unaccompanied version of "Bohemian Rhapsody," falsetto and all, the chances of it sounding anything like as tuneful as everyone singing together would be slim to none. It is a famously difficult song to sing with a huge range, a variety of rhythms, and the need for exceptional timing.

So how is it that thousands of individuals can somehow perform far more effectively than any individual among them? In the case of "Bohemian Rhapsody," it is likely to be a combination of a number of things. First, there are a small number of singers in the crowd who are good enough to sound great alone. These singers will sing every note correctly and keep in time. Less confident and competent singers will likely bail out on the toughest notes and follow the lead of those around them who are singing more proficiently on timing. In this way the good singers dotted throughout the crowd act like a series of strategically placed tuning forks, dragging everyone else a little closer to perfect pitch. Among the singers who do not have perfect pitch, many of them will be decent across a small range of notes. This means that at any point in the song the great singers will be bolstered by a large group of mediocre singers who are absolutely nailing that particular section of the track. Last, the bad singers who don't bail out when they can't make the note will all be bad in different ways. In other words, there is only one way to be in tune but many ways to be out of tune. This means that the bum notes won't dominate since there is not enough consistency among them to make anything other than an indistinct buzz of background noise that the crowd can easily tune out.

While the surprising musical superiority of the crowd may not have obvious applications to our success as a species, crowds can also outperform individuals in other important ways. For example, imagine you need to quickly make everyone in a group aware of a threat. Relying on each person to individually notice it is unlikely to be an effective strategy, and figuring out how to deliberately transmit the information in a coordinated way will inevitably take time. In crowds, however, because we are attuned to one another we tend to collectively focus on important information, such as a threat, faster than we would if each of us was acting alone. This is because of something called *gaze following*.[4] Rather than each person in the crowd continually scanning for new information, we look to the people around us and take our cues on what to look at based on how they are behaving. This means that if a few people in a crowd notice something important, those around them will quickly begin to focus on the same thing, triggering a process that captures the attention of the entire crowd very quickly.

Being able to sync with others in the crowd also has tactical advantages. For example, the phenomenon whereby crowds synchronize their footsteps, beginning to walk as one, seems to be something that happens in response to insufficient distance between pedestrians.[5] Moving into a collective stepping motion allows the crowd to keep moving forward while reducing the risk of dangerous collisions. Ironically, in some settings this collective stepping actually creates danger. For example, the power of the synchronized crowd caused the Millennium Bridge in London to wobble dramatically on its opening days.[6] There was nothing structurally wrong with the bridge: it was designed to hold thousands of pedestrians at any given moment. It was not, however, designed to hold a single synchronized organism the size of a thousand pedestrians. Beyond matters of survival, becoming greater than our individual selves also has other advantages. Brokers whose trades are synchronized with others earn more in the stock market,[7] and musicians play better as a group because they are attuned to complex feedback loops and cues among one another.[8] There are, of course, also downsides. Crowds can stampede and crush, and groupthink can take over when we try and make decisions as a collective.

So far, this chapter has been limited to simple actions performed by crowds: singing songs, stepping in time, or looking the same way. But crowds also mobilize in complex ways that have far longer-lasting effects. To examine how this happens, come with me on a brief trip to 1968 in the English fishing port of Hull.

The city was finally starting to get back on its feet after being the most heavily bombed place in the country after London in the Second World War. For those who worked in fishing, the strengthening economy would not have meant overnight prosperity. While the owners of the trawling companies—who stayed with their feet firmly on dry land and their eyes on the bottom line—got richer, the workers would have seen little of the gains. Most notably, trawling remained perilously dangerous. Over 150 years of operation, 900 boats had set sail and never come back, and with them 6,000 men. And Hull's trawlers had a mortality rate seventeen times higher than the men fifty miles to the south who worked in coal mining. But, even in a context where tragedy was the norm, the start of 1968 was horrific. Over just three weeks, three trawlers were lost at sea. Fifty-eight men, almost all of them from one small community, disappeared with the boats, leaving those behind devastated. As the details of the tragedies emerged, it became clear that the lack of basic protections for those on board was to blame. Weak communication protocols meant it took two weeks for the *St Romanus*, the first boat to go down, to be officially declared missing. In the meantime, the *Kingston Peridot* sunk off the northeast coast of Iceland, weighed down by ice on her deck and battered by storms. The news of her demise arrived in Hull one week after the crew of the last boat, the *Ross Cleveland*, set sail on the same course. Oblivious to the fate of their colleagues, they, along with two other vessels, went down in another northeast Icelandic storm.

There had been campaigns to change the working conditions of fishermen before, but they had failed to gain traction. This time, though, things were different. The tragedy in Hull took the debate out of the realm of trade unions and into the public eye. And it activated a new type of campaigner: the fishermen's wives.

Hull was a traditional place. Men went to sea and their wives were left behind raising children, working in jobs deemed acceptable for ladies, and generally keeping their heads down. For the residents of Hessle Road, 1968 was a far cry from the liberation of the swinging sixties of Carnaby Street. So when "Big" Lil Bilocca—a cod skinner whose father, son, and husband all worked at sea—got arrested trying to stop undercrewed trawlers from leaving St. Andrew's Dock, people paid attention. This brush with the police only seemed to fuel Lil's fire. Together with three other women—Christine Jensen, Mary Denness, and Yvonne Blenkinsop—she rallied hundreds of local women to march on the offices of Hull's trawler owners. The national press descended on the city and, because of the fashion of the time, dubbed the women the "Headscarf Revolutionaries." Some of the men supported these efforts, but many were horrified. Having women take charge of their safety was emasculating and embarrassing. Big Lil received death threats, lost her job, and was blacklisted from the fishing industry. Yvonne Blenkinsop, a cabaret singer by trade, was punched in the face by a man after giving a speech. But this didn't stop them. Together, the women drew up a charter demanding a long list of practical changes to make the trawlers safer. In less than two weeks they gathered 10,000 signatures. A petition, ample media coverage, and a threat to picket Prime Minister Harold Wilson's private residence, landed Lil—a woman who worked on the same street as the house she was born in—a meeting with the prime minister at 10 Downing Street. There, Wilson and his ministers acquiesced to every one of their requests. By May 1969, the trawler industry had been over-hauled. The design of vessels was more tightly regulated, high-quality safety equipment was mandatory, and legal standards were in place for radio operators, equipment, and reporting protocols. Mary Denness said, "We have achieved more in six weeks than the politicians and trade unions have in years," and she wasn't wrong. The Headscarf Revolutionaries were responsible for one of the most effective civil movements of twentieth-century Britain. But what was it that allowed them to succeed where others had failed?

Damon Centola, an academic at the University of Pennsylvania whose title curiously links communication, sociology, and engineering, would likely say that the fact the Headscarf Revolutionaries were ordinary people was critical.[9] Centola's research uses data to build an empirical picture of how social networks activate and drive change. For example, Centola simulates the way behavior spreads through networks under different conditions, seeking to understand why some things take off so spectacularly while most equally worthy movements fail to spark. The way we tell stories of social change usually suggests that there was one leader reacting to some event, one switch that got activated and somehow lit everyone else up. But a core finding of Centola's work is that multiple nodes in the network need to be activated if a behavior is to spread. To understand this, imagine a thousand candles: 999 of them are packed in tight; they represent the crowd. One larger candle stands a little apart; it represents an authority figure or a leader. If you light the single larger candle, it can burn but the flame won't spread because it is too distant from the rest of the candles. This is what happens when authority figures speak up in some circumstances:

they demand change, but there isn't a way to amplify their demands enough to grab attention. This is what happened in 1960s Britain. The trade unions were negotiating hard for changes to worker protections at sea, but they couldn't capture the latent potential for action among the people affected. Those people had their employers to keep happy and didn't see any chance that things would change even if they did speak up. Now imagine, instead, that one or more of the smaller candles is lit. The flame spreads out in concentric circles to the surrounding candles, quickly lighting all 999 wicks.

This is what happened when the triple trawler tragedy hit Hull. The news grabbed attention: people were listening in a way they had not before, and it pushed those who cared out of silence and into action. First people noticed that Big Lil lit up but so too had Christine, Mary, and Yvonne. Each of them covered a slightly different part of the network and enabled the flame to spread faster, activating 10,000 angry protesters who could not be ignored. Similarly, during the Arab Spring protests in the early 2010s, high-profile figures across North Africa and the Middle East were already speaking out against their governments, but ordinary people couldn't take their lead from them. They were too distant, and it was too risky to be a follower. When their peers began to organize, though, thousands of people took to the streets. Just like the candles, lots of small movements in the densest parts of the network are more effective than one call to action at the top of the social hierarchy. In the case of the Berlin Wall, too, people took to the streets because that's what their friends were doing. It wasn't that they didn't want the wall to come down—they did—but the motivation they needed to make it happen was locked up in their perception of what was socially acceptable. Usually, if someone transgresses a norm or rule, they are punished. If they break a law, such as trying to cross the wall, this punishment is enacted by the authorities. But if they breach a social norm, their peers hold them to account. This social feedback happens because it is in the interests of the herd to protect the invisible contract that holds society together. This can stall progress and disincentivize the act of questioning the status quo. At its worst, it can lead to large groups of people going along with a tide of atrocity. When there is enough latent discontent, though, the transgressors inspire others to follow, even when it might be dangerous to do so. Big Lil was still punished in an official sense when she was blacklisted by the fishing industry, but that didn't stop her from drumming up the 10,000 signatures she needed to get the government's attention.

Although the models are still relatively new, work like Centola's can help us improve our responses to everything from traffic management to epidemic control by giving more accurate predictions on the ways large groups of people might react. They reveal the invisible forces that shape our decisionscapes by showing how information, beliefs, and the behavior of those around us change our perspectives. Part IV explores this in more detail. Our decisionscapes are framed by extraneous factors. Just as an artist's work reflects the world they are working in, our judgments are products of our contexts.

IV THE FRAME

I have one language. It is not my own.
—Jacques Derrida[1]

15   ABOUT TIME

The clock made possible a temporal environment that is spatial, quantitative, fast paced, efficient and predictable. . . . A dial and hand translated the movement of time into movement through space. It made time into something divisible and concrete. Physical clock time metered out seconds, minutes, hours and days. It made it possible for people to schedule effectively and to measure periods of time with precision. By supplanting nature and God with clocks, and watches, mechanical time replaced religious and natural authorities for dividing up the day.
—Roger Neustadter[1]

In 2011, I did the Run to the Beat half-marathon in London. As I crossed the finish line, I checked my watch: *one hour, fifty-nine minutes, and seventeen seconds.* I was elated: after more failed attempts than I care to remember, I had finally cracked the elusive two-hour mark. It's not an especially fast time, but it was one that made me incredibly proud. That night, though, the official results went up. I searched my name and stared at the screen: *Elspeth Kirkman, two hours and eight seconds.* The elation evaporated. I do not exaggerate when I say I cried until I fell asleep, not a good move for someone as dehydrated as I was. Is this embarrassing to admit? Sure. But it gives a good insight into how much significance we attach to temporal milestones. I had worked hard to try and get in under two hours, and when the moment came I missed my goal by less than ten seconds. It was somehow worse than when I'd missed the two-hour mark by four minutes three weeks earlier.

My obsession with the two-hour mark is not unique. Take any long-distance race and graph the results. Some people will finish fast, some slow; most will finish within an hour of the average time. But if you zoom in on the "milestone" times—four hours in the marathon, for instance—you will see odd blips in the bell curve (figure 15.1).[2]

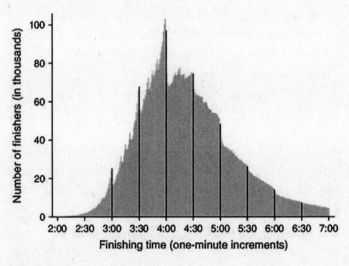

Figure 15.1
Graphed results of marathon race finish times.

As the vertical black lines on the graph show, more people than you would expect based on the rest of the data cross the line in the minutes before and after hour and half-hour finish times. It's like these temporal milestones are magnetic, dragging people over the line faster than they might cross it otherwise or pulling some people back like an invisible force.

Deadlines have a similar magnetism. In all kinds of scenarios, data show that people tend to wait until the last minute to complete a task on a deadline. This can be efficient. After all, if you're trying to do the best job possible—say, on a job application—you would want to maximize the time available to improve the quality. But studies show this is not what is happening. We often take the deadline to be a signal of how much work ought to be done to complete the task.[3] If, instead, we separated out the questions of what it would take to get the work done and how to fit in that work before the task is due, we might just find ourselves being more productive and less stressed.

The siren songs of deadlines and round numbers can call in all kinds of unexpected ways. They warp the temporal axis of our decisionscapes, causing distortions in our judgments. For example, many people use a financial product called a target retirement fund as a way of saving.[4] Target retirement funds are clever and convenient. You simply choose when you want to retire, join the fund along with many others around your age, and the fund manager looks after the rest. As your retirement date draws near, the fund manager will transition the investment portfolio out of riskier assets such as shares and into more stable bets such as bonds. Assuming you pick the right target retirement date, you should benefit from the lowered cost of going in with a lot of other investors and the expert steering of the fund as you prepare to enter retirement.

There are, though, two problems that undermine the effectiveness of target retirement funds. First, the funds themselves are an interesting example of how the arbitrary temporal milestones we create shape the world. To ensure there is enough buying power to make these funds cost-effective, they are generally set to target retirement dates every five years. For example: 2020, 2025, and 2030 would all have been investment options for those looking to buy into a fund. This means that people whose retirement year does not end in zero or five must decide whether they want to round up or down when choosing a fund. The dashed line on the graph in figure 15.2 shows what you would expect to happen: investors round up or

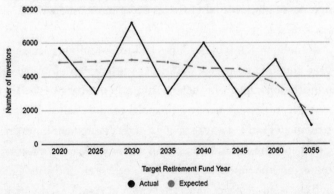

Expected Investment Patterns vs Actual Investment Patterns

Figure 15.2

Graphical representation of investment patterns in target retirement funds. Adapted from Liu, Xiao, Wei Zhang, and Ajay Kalra, "The Costly Zero Bias in Target Retirement Fund Choice," SSRN (2018), https://ssrn.com/abstract =3214811.

down to choose the fund that tracks closest to their retirement date. The line is smooth. The hard, jagged, line, on the other hand, shows what actually happens. Future retirees overinvest in funds that target years ending in zero and underinvest in those targeting years ending in five. This has a big effect. Imagine two people planning to retire at age seventy. One is born in 1968, meaning she will celebrate her seventieth birthday in 2038. Since she does not want to work beyond seventy, she should round down, targeting the 2035 retirement fund. Her assets will spend longer invested in stable but low-return bonds than someone a little older, but she will still benefit from the product. If, however, she displays a zero bias, she will round way down and choose the 2030 fund. This means her total saving period is shorter, meaning higher payments each month or less saved overall. It also means that her investments will spend a full eight years with no prospect of a high return. By contrast, someone born two years later, in 1970, will invest in the 2040 fund. Compared to our first investor, they will have longer to keep contributing to the fund, and they will benefit from the portfolio's risk profile being adjusted at a rate better suited to their actual retirement date.

When it comes to age, the zero bias is seductive in other ways too. When a milestone birthday appears on the horizon, we tend to change the way we make decisions about the biggest aspects of our lives. Twenty-nine-year-olds, for example, are more likely to have babies, get married, or buy a house than their twenty-eight- or thirty-year-old peers.[5] This suggests, to me at least, that we should beware the pull of the temporal milestone. A rushed engagement or overextending on a mortgage, for example, have predictable consequences. But other research suggests that something else might be going on. In another study, people at milestone ages such as thirty or forty years old were more likely to consider their overall achievements to date when considering life satisfaction.[6] People at less meaningful ages were shorter-sighted, using their immediate emotional state as the barometer of satisfaction, for instance. This suggests that temporal milestones provide some impetus for us to change our construal level, pulling back to see the big picture instead of tunneling in on quotidian detail. If this is the case, then perhaps the advent of a significant birthday gives us the push we need to assess what really matters to us and to commit in a way that shores up the future we want. Either way, with stake this high, it seems worth taking some time to pause and reflect in these milestone moments: Are we sure that what we are doing is in line with what we want? Or are our decisionscapes simply experiencing a temporary disruption?

We are puppeteered by the invisible strings of reified time every moment of every day. In most Western societies, we now live on what is known as *clock time*, where we organize our lives around evenly spaced temporal intervals as defined by the clock to impose order and consistency.[7] Of course, there is nothing natural about this, and for most of human history we have lived instead on *event time*; a task ended when you internally sensed it was finished, and you ate lunch when you were hungry, not when your calendar issued a pop-up to tell you your twenty-minute lunch window had started. This causes low-key chaos every single day: you can't catch the elevator around the hour marks in a workday as everyone begins a mass migration to their next meeting; you spend rush hour ensconced in the armpit of a stranger as everyone treks into work at once; and heaven help you if one of your precisely scheduled tasks runs into a delay. Occasionally we take a break—all at the same time, of course—from this madness. Set-piece events like Christmas act as annual temporal milestones that command all kinds of wild behavior. In many cultures, for example, we spend enormous amounts of money in holiday periods on gifts people do not want and on food that will ultimately go to waste. In a gloriously bah-humbug paper from 1993 called "The Deadweight Loss of Christmas," economics professor Joel Waldfogel estimated that gift-giving alone leads to between $4 and $13 billion in economic waste each year.[8] If an alien, unfamiliar with the ways of earthlings, asked us to explain how this is justifiable, I suspect we could just about make a case for the intangible social value of gift-giving and get away with it. But what we do next in this festive season is indefensibly bananas. In the dead zone between December 26 and January 1, we eat ourselves silly, drink to excess, spend too much time indoors, and wait until the stroke of midnight on New Year's Eve to perform a complete and very short-lived transformation into a better person. It is no wonder our resolutions are destined to fail.

Living by the clock, a way of life propagated to help improve wage efficiency by paying workers by the hour, also fools us into sleepwalking through time without really thinking about how we are spending it. The arbitrary division of time into a seven-day cycle alters the way we organize our lives. Schools and many jobs, for example, run during the week and break on weekends. This pattern has knock-on effects on the economy, our social lives, and even when we eat and sleep. This temporal architecture imprints on our psyche and changes the way we perceive the world, sometimes in surprising ways. Research by Jet Sanders and Rob Jenkins, for example, shows that our risk tolerance varies depending on the day of the week.[9] If we are faced with choices that require us to factor in risk on Thursday, for example, we will typically choose a more cautious option than we might on a Monday. By comparing voting intentions to actual votes in Thursday elections, they show that this phenomenon can change the outcome. In the case of the Scottish independence referendum of 2014, the analysis shows that the proportion of yes votes in response to the question "Should Scotland be an independent country?" was 4 percent lower than it would likely have been had the vote taken place on a Monday. The difference wouldn't have been enough to sway the result in this case, but the temporally governed malleability of our risk appetite does raise interesting questions about when elections should be held: Should our most risk-hungry or most risk-averse self be the one invited into the voting booth?

So far, I have described time, or at least the way we conceptualize and express it, as something universal. This is an oversimplification. While most of the world is signed up to coordinated global time zones, standardized units of time, and the same kinds of devices to keep track, there are important differences across cultures and countries about how we conceptualize time. Many of these reveal themselves through the language we use. In Mandarin, for example, the progression of time is described vertically in contrast to the horizontal progression imagined in many Western languages. Speakers of the Aymara language, who typically live in the Bolivian Andes, gesture in front of them when speaking about the past and behind them when indicating the future. And bilinguals whose language abilities span time conceptions can flit between mental models. Space is also represented differently between languages. The 200 or so speakers of Kuuk Thaayorre, a Paman language spoken by the Aboriginal community of Pormpuraaw on the west coast of Australia's Cape York Peninsula, use cardinal directions to describe location.[10] Instead of using words like left and right, they use words that reference east or north. When a Thaayorre speaker is telling a story, they will change the direction of the gesture they use to indicate where events took place, showing the compass direction rather than simply using their own position as a reference point. Studies show that this sensitivity to orientation runs deep. Kuuk Thaayorre speakers represent timelines of events running east to west no matter their orientation when asked to perform the task, and they have an unusually strong ability to identify cardinal compass directions without any obvious visual clues. Differences like these raise interesting questions about the extent to which our experiences of the world and the choices we make are mediated by the language we speak. For example, if the Thaayorre language does not center its speakers when referring to space, does it reduce egocentrism?

These questions are not new—far from it. Sometime toward the middle of the thirteenth century, for example, the Holy Roman Emperor, Frederick II, became interested in finding out what language a child would come to speak if they were raised without ever hearing another person's voice. Frederick's interest was not unique. Nor was his implicit assumption that the children would reveal some innate language rather than staying mute. The question was also one of great theological importance since it hinted at the promise of a divine language—a language that would allow us to perfectly convey the fundamental essence of things. A language in which we could speak to God. Unfortunately, such a question is pretty much unanswerable. Raising a child in the absence of language would be close to impossible and, if it were done, it would be hugely cruel. More unfortunately still, though, Frederick II's other area of interest was conducting barbaric experiments on his subjects. This is a man who once put a prisoner in a cask and waited for him to die to see if he could observe the soul leaving the tiny hole he cut into the wood. In the hands of someone with the power and tastes of Frederick II, the effect of language deprivation on children was entirely answerable.

And so Frederick II took several babies and gave them to foster mothers with the instruction to "suckle and bathe and wash the children, but in no ways to prattle or speak with them." The foster mothers did as he said, raising the babies in total silence and without any other form of communication or human warmth. Frederick waited in suspense to see if the children would speak Hebrew, Greek, Latin, Arabic, the language of their birth parents, or something else entirely. Whichever it was, he imagined, would be the original Adamic language spoken in Eden. It was a question he would never answer: one by one, the children died, unable to live "without clappings of the hands, and gestures, and gladness of countenance, and blandishments."[11]

Frederick's failed experiment was not the last. In 1493, James IV of Scotland tried something similar, the results of which appear to have escaped the record. Like Frederick II, James's interest in language deprivation was of its time. By the end of the fifteenth century, the desire to find the Adamic language was still alive, although its focus had morphed a little. Now, theologians across Europe were interested in the extent to which speakers of different languages could absorb the Gospel. This interest was not academic; it was a critical part of the colonial playbook. Columbus was newly returned from the Americas, and the race was on between the European superpowers to find faster trade routes. To cut down on conflict, Pope Alexander VI issued a papal bull dividing the "non-Christian" lands of the New World between Spain and Portugal. Ships from each country set sail to find what their new territories had to offer, taking the Bible and their languages with them. Eventually, this colonial project would spawn a hierarchy of languages dictated entirely by the empire-builders. This hierarchy gave a proxy for their view of the savage and the refined; language was recruited as a tool of racism and xenophobia. And so, it is with the baggage of religion, colonialism, and notions of supremacy that modern scholars have gingerly taken on the current incarnation of the question: Do the languages we speak alter the way we think and behave?

In the (happy) absence of large-scale randomized language-deprivation experiments, it is very hard to prove or disprove whether the language itself influences behavior since languages are not independent from one another or from the cultures in which they are spoken. To take an example, let's say you wanted to demonstrate that people who speak languages with different second-person pronouns for formal and informal relationships have more hierarchical worldviews. It would be almost impossible to do this convincingly because more hierarchical societies are likely to use more hierarchical forms of address. This makes it very difficult to persuasively show that the language, and not the culture, is the key factor. Nowadays, we have the analytical tools needed to take the relationship between culture and language into account in this kind of research. For example, a few years ago academic research by M. Keith Chen at UCLA broke out of the ivory tower and into the public consciousness with a big claim: the language we speak influences how we prepare for events in the future.[12] Chen's insight exploited the fact that languages vary in the extent to which they differentiate between the present and the future. In German, for instance, saying, "It rains tomorrow" (*morgen regnet es*) clearly refers to a future event with no need for a distinct future tense. English, on the other hand, makes the distinction: "It will rain tomorrow." In the initial publication, Chen showed that speakers who separate the future and the present grammatically save less money, smoke more cigarettes, have more unprotected sex, and tend to be heavier. In other words, by distancing the future linguistically, they made it feel less important. The conclusion was infuriating to those who study the interrelated nature of languages as it did not consider these relationships. Rather than reject this criticism, Chen shared his data and teamed up with two of his naysayers, Seán G. Roberts and James Winters, to look deeper. They reran the analysis taking into account the way that languages are interrelated.[13] The result was surprising to Roberts and Winters. Their model did weaken the link between language and future-oriented behavior, but it didn't erase it. By one adjusted estimate, speakers of languages that clearly differentiate between the present and the future save at a rate that is 39 percent to 57 percent lower than their compatriots who do not make the linguistic distinction, for example.

As the research currently stands, it seems unlikely that the languages we speak alter our lives in meaningful ways. But the way we use specific parts of language can have important effects on our decisionscapes. The next chapter looks more closely at some of these.

16   THE PASSIVE VOICE WAS USED

The Hennepin County Government Center in Minneapolis looks as though it was designed by a Supervillain. Its steel-framed towers resemble a pair of twenty-four-story razors, connected by an elaborate network of glass catwalks. Together, they slice the letter "H" into the skyline. Inside the cold granite walls, though, is a microcosm of the human experience. People come to the building to register births, get married, report deaths, and seek refuge. It is a place of joy and grief, of fear and boredom; a secular temple to the bureaucracy that structures a life. Although it sounds unlikely, you may have seen the Hennepin County Government Center, although you almost certainly didn't register it at the time. It is the building where, in March 2021, Derek Chauvin was convicted for the murder of George Floyd.

The case was big. Almost a year earlier, people around the world had watched the footage of Chauvin kneeling on Floyd's neck, crushing his face into the tarmac for nine minutes. The video, or, more specifically, its depiction of the death of another Black man at the hands of police brutality, triggered a global wave of protests. Millions of people took to the streets demanding racial justice, and now they had their eyes on the court in Hennepin County. Before the trial could start, Derek Chauvin's defense lawyer pulled out. A new lawyer, Eric J. Nelson, a managing partner at a ten-person criminal defense firm in Minneapolis, took over. Nelson isn't what you picture when you imagine the defense attorney for the biggest case in the world. He wears a practical-looking sports jacket in his corporate photo, and his bio describes a strong track record on DUI offenses. Like all defense lawyers, he'll be used to getting heat, but this is an international media circus. Another local lawyer, Eric C. Nelson, posts this on his website: "NOTE: IF YOU ARE LOOKING FOR THE ERIC NELSON WHO IS REPRESENTING DEREK CHAUVIN, THAT'S NOT ME. YOU WANT [hyperlinked] THIS GUY. (Welcome to Minnesota, where the name Eric Nelson is as common as walleye sandwiches. I wish my parents had named me Thor instead. Then I wouldn't have this problem.)" I guess that gives some idea of the kind of correspondence the other Eric Nelson was receiving.

On March 29, 2021, Nelson gives his opening statement to the court from behind a plexiglass screen. It takes twenty-four minutes. During this time, he speaks calmly, reading from a stack of papers and stumbling only occasionally. He lays out a story that tracks the events of the day George Floyd died, introducing places and characters, foreshadowing important pieces of evidence, important moments of doubt. On eighteen separate occasions, he uses the phrase "you will learn" when addressing the jury, reinforcing the idea that—no matter how clear things seem—the work has not yet been done to draw a firm conclusion.[1] He is formal, factual, and generally unemotional in his delivery; Derek Chauvin is not a sympathetic figure, and Nelson knows it. In fact, Chauvin—the defendant, his client—is barely present in his words. He is mentioned by name just ten times, less than both Alexander Keung and Thomas Lane, colleagues of Nelson's who will stand trial that summer. George Floyd, on the other hand, is mentioned fifty-four times, although when Nelson reaches the moment that the urgency of Floyd's medical situation becomes clear, he pulls out of naming him: "They came, they picked up Mr. . . . Rather than attempting to resuscitate him or treat him on the scene, they loaded him into the ambulance." When he does reference him, it is as "Mr. Floyd" on all but one occasion. The honorific passes as a marker of respect but it also puts "Mr. Floyd" at a remove when compared to the familiar "Derek." In different ways, both Chauvin and Floyd are pushed into the background of their own story, minimized in the decisionscapes of those charged with judging the case.

There is another interesting feature of Nelson's account that seems designed to shape the perceptions of the jury at key moments: the use of the passive voice. As a reminder, since it has been a long time since most of us sat down for a grammar lesson, the active voice places the subject or agent of the sentence first and the object second. The line "Mr. Floyd banged his face into the plexiglass partition of the squad car" is written in the active voice: Mr. Floyd is the subject and his face the object. The passive voice, on the other hand, places the object first and may even fail to mention the subject altogether. For example, "Mr. Floyd was pronounced dead." Most style guides discourage the use of the passive voice in all but exceptional cases. One such exception is when you want to shift focus from one party onto another. For example, a style guide published by the City University of New York's law school advocates the use of the passive voice when "you want to play down the actor's role in the event. (For instance, maybe the actor is your client.) Example: When the lights went out, several punches were thrown."[2] CUNY is not alone in promoting the use of the passive voice as a device to pull focus or divert blame. A brief review of other guides to legal writing reveal that such advice is common. In other words, within the legal profession, there is explicit recognition that the passive voice creates a kind of psychological distance that benefits defendants: put glibly, the sentence used can change the sentence given. Back to Nelson, who—for the most part—avoids the passive voice. Just twenty-two sentences, around 8 percent of the total in the piece, are passive, and most of those do not relate to specific people. For example: "Chicago is considered a high crime area," and "Evidence must be looked at." There is one person that Nelson refers to almost exclusively in the passive voice, though: George Floyd. In the extract below, I have italicized three instances of the passive voice where Floyd is the object of the sentence:

> You will learn, ultimately, that *Mr. Floyd was transported* to the Emergency Department at Hennepin County efforts . . . where *efforts to save Mr. Floyd were made* at the direction of Dr. Bradford Wankhede Langenfeld. Again, he took important tests, he ran, uh, blood samples, and blood gas samples. He took certain . . . very important . . . obtained very important pieces of information. You will learn that later that evening, *Mr. Floyd was pronounced dead.*

Mr. Floyd, or—perhaps more accurately—Mr. Floyd's body, is grammatically objectified, acted upon; he does not go to the hospital of his own volition, he is not in control of the efforts to save his life, he is not the agent when it comes to his own death. In some ways, this presentation is fitting. After all, George Floyd did not ask for any of this. But the passive voice blunts the details of the most emotionally evocative aspects of the case. Like the use of "Mr.," it sounds respectful but at the same time it makes George Floyd seem more distant or abstract, hovering just above the situation as it unfolds.

The passive voice also allows Nelson to erase other people from the account. This isn't necessarily bad form. To an extent it doesn't matter who pronounced George Floyd dead or who drove him to hospital. But it does mean that the focus is on Floyd and not those who did this to him. It may sound like a stretch to claim this kind of thing matters, but research suggests otherwise. One neat study takes a very simple approach to answering the question whether we interpret the same information differently depending on whether it is presented in the active or passive voice.[3] Participants in the experiment were presented with one of two cues. The first version of the cue was written in the active voice and stated, "Red follows blue." The second gave the same description but in the passive voice: "Blue is followed by red." Participants were then asked to color in an empty rectangle using red and blue crayons in a way that represented what they read. Those who saw the active sentence typically covered more of the rectangle with red. Those who saw the passive sentence covered more of it with blue. In other words, the way the information was communicated altered perceptions of what it meant, with the passive voice minimizing the role of red, the subject of the sentence. If this is true for blocks of color, would it be true in a court of law? It certainly seems plausible. For example, in another study, when asked to describe what they saw in a video clip showing a rape, viewers were more likely to use the passive voice if they thought the victim was responsible for what happened.[4] These viewers also tended to more strongly believe that rapes can be provoked, for example, if a victim is wearing revealing clothing or if they had previously had sex with the assailant. There is also research that suggests the choice of active or passive language changes the interpretation of violence against women. Students assigned to read crime reports in the passive voice were more accepting of violence against women than their peers who saw the same reports in an active voice. Male students assigned to read the passive reports were likely to believe less harm was done to the victim and to assign less blame to the perpetrator.[5]

We know, by now, that distance is not inherently helpful or harmful. Just as the distancing properties of the passive voice can lead to worse outcomes, they can also be a force for good. In self-talk, for example, using the passive voice can improve performance on a task: "I will write this book" just seems less intimidating when expressed as "This book will be written!" Here the passive voice helps people maintain focus by centering the task and not the person enacting it; by reducing focus on yourself, you improve the odds that you get the job done. This is reinforced by the work of Ethan Kross at the University of Michigan. In several studies, Kross and colleagues test the effect of another distancing device: using the second or third person in self-talk, rather than "I." Just like the passive voice, using "you" (second person) or your own name (third person) improves our ability to regulate thoughts, feelings, and behavior in socially stressful situations. This doesn't just reduce anxiety; it also enhances performance.

For example, study participants who were rated on their social interactions and public-speaking abilities scored better when they had been told to reflect on their feelings using non-first-person pronouns or their own name.[6] The findings extend to other kinds of stress and anxiety. In another study, participants were asked to write about their fears in relation to a potential Ebola outbreak in the United States.[7] Those instructed to use their name—a third-person perspective—in place of "I" were better at rationalizing their fears and reported lower levels of concern. These differences are so subtle that we barely register them. They haunt the periphery of our consciousness, like ghosts in the machine of language. But they shape the way we perceive the events around us. This subtle curation of our decisionscapes is something like the role of composition in art. The artist does not accidentally litter the scene they are painting with random objects, or capture people unposed. Just like Eric Nelson, they are deliberate in their choices about what is presented, where it is placed, and how.

While lawyers, like Eric Nelson, use their time on the floor of the court to manipulate emotional distance through language, they do so in the context of judicial processes that are designed to create distance. This design choice is partly deliberate. Jurors are regular people being asked to make decisions using only the evidence presented. Without an environment and processes designed to tamp down extralegal factors, such as empathy for the defendant or their own personal experiences, they might make decisions that do not fairly reflect the "facts" of the case. The prompts to consider only the facts help jurors absolve themselves of guilt in difficult decisions. They also tend to take their lead from the environment, for example, adopting legal language to create emotional distance from the defendant and enhance "objectivity" in their decision processes. This process of distancing is more common when it comes to death penalty trials. For example, in a post-trial interview in Texas, one defendant—cited in research by Robin Conley—shows how legal language helps navigate a shift in emotional gears to construct empathetic distance: "it is very difficult to sit there and listen to someone's grey-haired old daddy beg you not to kill their boy. . . . However, the charge . . . every one of us, swore to, on . . . the day of our oath . . . said that we would only let evidence guide us. We would not let supposition, emotion, prejudice, I forget the other term but something like that, okay. So, you must try to put your emotion aside as much as you can and only go on what is presented as evidence."[8]

While this idea of only using the evidence provides a kind of moral protection for jurors, it is complicated by the fact that some kinds of sentences do demand consideration of wider contextual factors. In the capital murder cases Conley was studying in Texas, for example, jurors are asked two questions. First, whether the defendant poses a "continuing threat to society." And second, whether there is any circumstantial factor in the case "to warrant that a sentence of life imprisonment rather than a death sentence be imposed." If the jurors answer yes to the first question and no to the second, then the defendant is sentenced to receive a lethal injection. These questions are interesting in two ways. First, and most obviously, they never require the jurors to explicitly condemn someone to the death penalty. Second, though, they explicitly ask that the jurors make subjective judgments about the defendant and their wider circumstances. This means that the comfort jurors find in legal models that frame their decisions as being led by objective evidence is misplaced. Jurors feel this tension, and their language reveals a lot about how they negotiate it, creating and collapsing empathetic distance as they work through their decisions. Take this reflective statement from a juror who had voted in a way that led to a death sentence. The shift in perspective partway through this reflection is marked by the change in the words he uses to describe the defendant. When he discusses how you might see a murderer at a distance, he uses "that person" and says they should be "eliminated." But when he moves to the specifics of the case at hand he focuses on "Bobby," "a real human being":

it's not like anything I could have ever imagined because you read newspaper accounts or you watch on TV and you think, well that person, you know, they just need to be, you know, eliminated. And let me tell you, from the graphic pictures we saw, this would fall (laughing) in that category. But, you know, then you realize there's a real human being. Did he stumble, fall, and even if he did, just the mere fact of loading a shotgun and putting somebody in that position I mean is that, that's pretty serious! . . . it was very interesting to meet Bobby, and he's a very gentle soul, and we, as Bobby says, we're two sides of the same coin. We were educated probably within a mile and a half of each other. And, you know, we knew the same streets and things like that. When you start talking about it it's like frightening (laughing) how close we all are. And this is as far as you think two people would be. But then you start to see the similarities. That's truly interesting.

Defendants themselves can also use language as a tool of persuasion. In fact, those who are most persuasive may be least likely to truly repent for their crimes. Psychopaths differ from the general population on a few important cognitive, social, and emotional dimensions. They are unusually self-centered, lack depth in their emotional experiences, struggle with behavioral control, and do not experience moral sensibility. Beneath the surface, they also look different than the average person. Brain scans show that those with a diagnosis of psychopathy have less gray matter in key areas of the brain, such as the frontal lobe, which is associated with emotional regulation and impulse control, and the temporal lobe, which is implicated in recognizing and using language. These differences do not obviously impair cognitive performance. In fact, psychopaths can excel in their use of language, using their words to charm and manipulate others for their own gain. One study on Canadian offenders, for example, showed that those with a diagnosis of psychopathy are more than twice as likely than those without such a diagnosis to be granted parole, a process that requires them to make a persuasive application.[9] This is especially surprising given psychopaths are more likely to reoffend than non-psychopaths. But although psychopaths do not score differently on regular cognitive tests, the story changes when it comes to a forensic examination of the way they use language.

In one study, fifty-two convicted murderers were asked to give an account of their crime.[10] Some had a diagnosis of psychopathy, and some did not. The accounts were then transcribed so that they could be processed by text analysis software. The software identified specific differences in the way psychopaths and non-psychopaths told their stories. For example, psychopaths used more past tense verbs in their narratives. The researchers take this to signal greater detachment from the incident: for the psychopaths these events are distant, in the past, forgotten, while the consequences of crimes are still present for non-psychopaths.

In this chapter I have shown that *how* we talk about something frames our decisionscapes. But sometimes we want to avoid talking directly about something altogether. In these cases, there are plenty of other linguistic devices that allow us to make no direct mention of the thing we are talking about, excluding it from the frame entirely. The next chapter looks at the effect of three such devices: euphemism, metaphor, and metonymy.

17 BEATING ABOUT THE BUSH, AND OTHER EUPHEMISMS

There is at least one thread on Netmums.com asking for advice on what to call an infant daughter's genitals. The suggestions are forthcoming: *bits, china, down below, fanny, floof, flower, foo foo, front bits, front bum, lala, mary, meemee, minky, minnie, moo, nin-nin, noo noo, parts, pee pee, privates, sassy, secrets, tuppence, twinkie, twinkle, twizzle,* and—although I reckon this user was having a laugh—*v-jay-jay.* The thread makes me wonder about the messages we send our children when we refuse to call a vulva a vulva (an issue the Swedes overcame by inventing a new name for a female child's genitals in 2006: *snippa,* a feminine variant of the male equivalent, *snopp*).[1] It can't be nothing: after all, for most grown adults, even saying the word *vulva* feels uncomfortable. We would rather use a euphemism, holding our bodies at a figurative distance, behind glass, only to be broken out in an emergency.

It isn't just vulvas. We use euphemistic and metaphorical language to distance ourselves from all kinds of discomfort. In English (with thanks to the Normans for bringing Old French to our shores) the meat on our tables doesn't evoke the animal in the field. Pork, beef, and mutton allow us to enjoy meals without thoughts of the mortal and visceral. Indeed, whenever something difficult comes up in conversation, we can rest assured that euphemism or censorship will come to the rescue. When someone dies, they pass. And, when it comes to illness, we haven't advanced since Franz Kafka wrote, as he lay dying in a sanatorium, "verbally I don't learn anything definite, since in discussing tuberculosis . . . everybody drops into a shy, evasive, glassy-eyed manner of speech."[2] In our day-to-day, euphemisms are a welcome feature of our language. They allow us to be sensitive and avoid conflict. But their distancing effect is not without cost. Euphemisms can be pernicious. They make it even harder to talk about our most painful and human experiences. So hard, in fact, that we may think it better not to talk about them at all.

In 2013, Lulu Wang's mother called her with the news that Nai Nai, her grandmother, had incurable lung cancer. At the end of the call, she made one thing very clear: under no circumstances was Nai Nai to find out. In Wang's semi-autobiographical film, *The Farewell*, the fictionalized version of Lulu's mother explains, "When people get cancer, they die. But it's not the cancer that kills them, it's the fear." In other words, the justification for not telling Nai Nai about her diagnosis is that the word *cancer* is powerful enough to kill. Wang, who lives in the United States, learned that her experience is surprisingly common. It is routine in China, where her Nai Nai lives, for family members to manage the communication between a loved one and their doctor. In a 2018 survey, 82 percent of Chinese physicians said they would not tell a patient they had cancer if doing so went against the wishes of a family member.[3]

Even if the patient was a member of the physician's own family, half of the doctors surveyed would choose not to tell them it was cancer (although just 19 percent would want to be kept in the dark themselves). The idea that not sharing the diagnosis could be physically protective seems like magical thinking. After all, a disease of the body should, in theory, be immune to the words used to describe it. But perhaps we shouldn't be so quick to dismiss the idea that the language surrounding a disease matters. Research shows that, when cancer is portrayed using metaphors of enmity, we tend to see preventive behaviors as less effective and less appealing.[4] We feel as though we have no agency over the fate of our own bodies; the "invasion" is inevitable, "the battle" unwinnable, so why bother trying to avoid it? Such metaphors can also be harmful to those who have cancer. War metaphors like this imply that, with enough strategy and resilience, the patient might have control over whether they "win." If they decline treatment, they are seen to "surrender," perhaps even letting down their loved ones who expect them to "fight." The word *cancer* might not be able to hurt us, but the way we talk about it can.

It isn't just cancer. Metaphors that move us are everywhere. We change the way we think lawbreakers should be dealt with based on how crime is described. When it is a "beast" that "lurks" and "preys" on the community, we tend to think harsher enforcement is the answer. When the same crime is presented as a "virus" that "infects" and "plagues," we favor treating root causes, such as poverty, unemployment, and inadequate healthcare.[5] When asked how they formed their view, participants in this research barely mentioned the use of metaphor, especially not as an influential factor in their assessment. Instead, they reported that the facts and figures—which are identical in both metaphorical frames—had persuaded them. This is especially remarkable as the metaphorical frame had a greater effect than their existing political beliefs: in other words, the metaphor used could be more influential than your voting record when it comes to determining support for the police or better health-care access.

Metaphors can also exaggerate social distance. For example, in an interview in 2015, the British Prime Minister David Cameron referred to migrants as "a swarm of people coming across the Mediterranean."[6] His remarks sparked a heated debate in the British press about whether this dehumanizing language was deliberate or appropriate, and whether it even mattered. Whatever Cameron's intentions, the "human as animal" trope comes with a long and malicious history. In Nazi Germany, the propaganda publication *Der Stürmer* variously portrayed Jews as vermin, worms, parasites, serpents, beasts, and livestock.[7] This kind of metaphor is powerful because it places two important weights on the scale of public opinion. First, it firmly establishes the difference between "us"—the civilized readers—and "them," the vermin invaders. Individual humans fleeing persecution become a block of unwelcome strangers. Second, these metaphors stigmatize the group they describe. They make them seem base, unclean, and subhuman. Research shows that using vermin metaphors to describe immigrants induces disgust and increases support for harsh immigration measures, especially among those with a strong national identity.[8] Any last wisp of compassion is extinguished by a seemingly innocuous choice of words. Dehumanizing language also has an effect on the immigrants it is used to describe.

In a study conducted by Mona El-Hout and Kristen Salomon, immigrants who read an article using animalistic metaphors for migrants showed higher cardiovascular stress responses and longer recovery times than those who read a similar article that used criminal metaphors.[9]

Where metaphor gives the illusion of bridging the gap between things that are not obviously alike, such as vermin and immigrants, metonymy brings adjacent concepts closer together. Metonymy is the literary device by which an example of a category becomes representative of the category itself. For example, a "suit" is something worn by businessmen, but at some point it became a shorthand for the businessman himself. Metonymy makes the abstract more concrete by substituting a specific feature for the whole. This can have the effect of making things feel more psychologically proximal. In psychology this is reminiscent of a phenomenon known as the *identifiable victim effect*.[10] Several studies show that giving an individual example of something—for example, a child affected by famine—makes people more likely to take an action, like donating to charity, than if they saw information about the larger context. On the face of it this doesn't make sense: if we are moved by one starving child, we should be more moved by learning there are thousands of starving children. But the wider statistic is too big and too abstract for us to comprehend. In this case metonymy eliminates distance, making sure we are appropriately struck by the gravity of the situation.

By drawing a comparison between two things, metaphor can create a sense of familiarity, bringing new concepts into our existing frame of reference. Similarly, by collapsing a more complex concept into a single object, metonymy simplifies what we are looking at, making it easier to process. Both these devices can have a stress-reducing effect by making us feel like we can hold new ideas in mind easily or tether them back to concepts we are already comfortable with. The next chapter looks at what happens when we encounter new information that cannot be accommodated by our existing worldview.

18   BREAKING THE FRAME

People laughed when I said I wanted to be a comedian.
They're not laughing now.
—Bob Monkhouse, comedian[1]

Humor works because it subverts our expectations. In the early eighteenth century, German philosopher Arthur Schopenhauer said, of humor, that "the cause of laughter in every case is simply the sudden perception of the incongruity between a concept and the real objects which have been thought through it in some relation, and laughter itself is just the expression of this incongruity."[2] Although he doesn't use this language, what he is describing is a sudden shift in construal level. As a reminder, things construed at a high level are abstract and distant. Things construed at a low level are concrete, specific, and psychologically proximal. As Schopenhauer has it, the shock of the contrast between the concrete and the abstract is what makes us laugh. It isn't just humor; much of what we find entertaining also operates by exploiting a gap between what we expect and what we get. Detective novels have unexpected solutions, ghost stories are suspenseful because we cannot predict what will happen, and fantasy creates worlds with unfamiliar rules that reduce our ability to guess what might come next. But most of the time when expectations and reality do not match, we are far from entertained. In fact, William Hazlitt, reflecting around the same time as Schopenhauer, considered this to be part of the fundamental human experience: "Man is the only animal that laughs and weeps: for he is the only animal that is struck with the difference between what things are, and what they ought to be."[3]

So how is it that we delight in some bucked expectations and despair in others? We are powerful prediction machines, endlessly forecasting out a range of possible outcomes and planning for the most likely set of scenarios. When something unexpected yet predictable in hindsight—like the punch line or the plot twist—crops up, it is as if the whole frame of our decisionscape has been momentarily widened. When we don't have to suffer the consequences of this in a meaningful way, it thrills us. The punch line of a joke and the denouement of a plot point both bring relief through clarity. They don't force us to question our fundamental worldview so we can easily square our new interpretation of the information we saw—be it a joke setup or a character arc—with the surprising revelation at the end. The trouble comes when we *do* have to suffer the consequences of the gap between expectations and reality. Unexpected events blow open uncomfortable questions like: "If I didn't see this coming, what else am I missing?" This can be minor. For example, situations in which we do not get closure can be disproportionately frustrating even when they are trivial. Think of Andy Warhol's 1965 film *Empire*. It is an eight-hour, slow-motion shot of the Empire State Building. When you view *Empire* in a gallery, you are told explicitly that nothing happens. And yet many people find themselves sitting on uncomfortable museum benches for minutes on end watching, their expectations frustrated by the unfulfilled promise of the medium: a narrative.

Psychologists have been interested for some time in why we crave reconciliation and closure so deeply. The answer, it seems, has to do with our need for a stable sense of meaning in our world. Our decisionscapes need to make sense to us, to have some unifying themes and styles. But when contradictory information is introduced, it is as though a new part of the frame opens up, showing us something we had not previously known we needed to accommodate in our *mental model* of the world. When this happens, we seek to preserve our meaning model through some specific mental processes. In a series of studies led by Travis Proulx, psychologists exposed research subjects to stimuli that could plausibly disrupt their meaning model, for example, showing them absurdist art or asking them to read a short story by Franz Kafka.[4] When compared to subjects who had not seen these stimuli, these people were more likely to express a need for structure and to be better at learning to recognize new patterns. While the effects of absurdist art are small, the insights from this work might explain some of how major social changes play out. For example, when social or economic progress accelerates, we often see two contrasting reactions. Some people double down on the status quo, fetishizing its structure and familiarity. Others, though, find a new kind of creativity unleashes, enabling them to see things in a completely different light. Kafka and others are examples of this latter camp. Modernism emerged as an artistic and philosophical response to the seismic shifts of the late nineteenth and early twentieth centuries. For example, instability in Spain gave us Dalí, Picasso, and García Lorca. And the urgent need to rebuild cities after the destruction of World War II accelerated the adoption of modern architecture.

Such periods of instability also do something else. They reveal and challenge the invisible curation of choice that scaffolds our lives. Just as we might bound the choices we offer to a toddler—"Would you like bubbles or no bubbles?" rather than asking them if they'd like a bath, for example—the choices we see are edited by external forces in ways we rarely notice. But sometimes something happens to change this. The strain of World War II, for example, put women all over the world into jobs they had previously been discouraged from. Ordinary women worked in factories and played professional sport in stadiums. Princess Elizabeth, the future Queen of England, became a truck mechanic. When the war ended, some of the previous social order was restored, but the collective decisionscape had changed to accommodate the idea that women could contribute to society in more ways than they had previously been allowed to. Even without global shocks, like war, there are reliable ways to force the expansion of our decisionscapes. The *radical flank effect* is a social psychology term that describes the phenomenon whereby a faction willing to take extreme action on an issue makes those with more moderate views look more sensible.[5] This can mean that issues that have failed to gain traction can benefit greatly from a radical flank grabbing public attention. Most social movements have radical and moderate flanks. Feminism, civil rights, and labor movements have all progressed enormously in the last century and have done so through mainstreaming of their core issues. This mainstreaming has, in part, been enabled by radical flanks that have grabbed newspaper headlines and stretched the public imagination on the reference window these issues sit within.

The bounded nature of our decisionscapes can also affect our decisions and judgments on an individual level. For example, think back to Katie, the social worker who was using the "perfect match" as the comparison when placing siblings for adoption. Because, like all of us, her decisionscape was bounded, she found herself making the wrong comparison: using perfection as a benchmark instead of the reality of the current situation for those kids. Unrealistic comparisons are not the only issue we encounter when part of the information we need to make a decision is not in the frame. Often we find that, when faced with missing information, we fill in the blanks with an imagined piece of information. This can be trivial, but it can also have an impact on important decisions. Take, for example, "ban the box" policies in many US states. These policies make it illegal for employers to ask applicants about their criminal record before offering them a job. The box in question is the checkbox on the hiring form. These policies seem smart on the face of it. After all, if someone has served their time and has no further restrictions on their activities, they should not be discriminated against in the labor market. The box penalizes those with records: they either lie on the form or face being screened out without ever being considered. Banning the box means they get a fair shot. As more and more states embraced banning the box, though, Jennifer Doleac and Benjamin Hansen started to wonder if the absence of a box made employers more likely to guess who might have a record and reject those people as a precaution.[6] By analyzing recruitments in states with ban the box in place, they uncovered a serious unintended consequence of the policy: ban the box is harmful to young Black men applying to low-skill jobs. In fact, where ban the box is in place, these young men are 5 percent less likely to be employed than they would be otherwise. When information that employers consider to be important—in this case, whether an applicant has a criminal record—is not included, they use population-level information—in this case, the fact that criminal record rates are higher among young Black men in low-skilled roles—to try and eliminate the risk they will make an offer to someone who turns out to have a conviction.

In this section, I looked at the forces that build the invisible frame that bounds our decisionscapes. In many ways, this frame is our greatest threat. It constrains our options and our ability to appraise them, and no individual action is enough to break free of it. There will always be a frame. In complex societies, we need superstructures and governing bodies to order our lives. But the way the frame is constructed, the values applied, the choices made, matters greatly.

In the final chapter of this book, I look at how the makers of the frame have their own decisionscapes, and how understanding their own perspectives and limitations can help us tackle one of the greatest challenges facing our world: human-made climate change.

CONCLUSION: DESIGNING THE DECISIONSCAPE

Most of this book has focused on individual decisionscapes—that is, the unique way that each of us forms a perspective on the world around us, and the effects that has on our judgment. But, as the later chapters have shown, not everything about our decisions is in our control. Before we even begin to contemplate our choices, the decisionscape is constrained and framed. But the actions of the media, governments, corporations, and others with a hand in designing the paradigm of our lives are also determined by human decision-makers with their own incentives and agendas. To drive change at the systemic level, improving the options available to each of us individually, we need to understand these institutional decisionscapes, what constrains them, and how they can be influenced.

In part 1, "Distance and Diminution," I explored the different facets of psychological distance. I showed that we use temporal, spatial, social, and hypothetical distance to assess the options available to us. The effect of this is that the more distant something feels, the less of a bearing it will have on our decisions. Right now, at least for most of us in the Global North, climate change is distant on every dimension. It happens in the future, to other people, and in faraway places. On the axis of hypothetical distance, climate crisis is hard for us to imagine since we have no point of reference. It doesn't matter that it is, at our current rate of resource consumption, inevitable: we simply can't fathom it. And so we engage in extreme diminution, minimizing the problem by shoving it into the background of life's day-to-day concerns. This is not just an individual issue; for governments, too, the timeline of climate change is incompatible with the timeline of politics. Climate investments don't pay off within a political cycle, and, worse, the best outcome—averted disaster—is invisible. Invisible results don't win elections. One way around this is to legislate to protect the future. For instance, in 2015 Wales passed the Well-being of Future Generations Act, which legally binds public bodies in Wales to act with the interests of future generations in mind. For example, the legislation led to the government canceling plans to build a new motorway and freezing planning for new roads in favor of investing in public transport and active travel. Legislation like this gets politicians off the hook to some extent. It becomes easier to take potentially unpopular future-focused decisions when you can point to a legal obligation hanging over you.

In part 2, "Viewpoint," I showed how vested interest affects our decisionscapes, how our identities act like lenses on the world, and how those identities can be shifted by the behavior of those around us. The problem with climate change is that it is in no one's immediate interests to tackle it. Individually, we benefit from unconstrained consumption and take almost no rap for consuming at an unsustainable rate, so expecting people to sacrifice immediate pleasure for some abstract future gain that won't necessarily accrue to them is magical thinking. One way governments can intervene is to correct market prices to reflect the hidden environmental costs of goods and services. This might sound regressive, but it can be done in a way that rewards those who constrain their consumption. In Canada, for example, the federal government imposes a carbon tax on fuel but then gives the money raised back to its people in the form of a rebate. Since the rebate is a fixed amount but the amount of tax you pay is based on the fuel you consume, those who use less fuel can end up receiving more money than they ever spent. It's not just fuel; there are many goods and services whose price is artificially low because the polluting effects of production are not captured in it. Livestock farming, for example, is the world's single largest producer of greenhouse gases. According to research led by Franziska Funke, correcting the price of beef to reflect these costs would lead to an increase of between 35 percent and 55 percent.[1] If governments were more bullish on beef, pricing meat products to reflect their true costs, consumers would reduce their demand and the additional revenues raised could pay for development of new alternative products, subsidize lower-carbon foods, or simply be returned as they are in Canada.

In part 3, "Composition," I discussed the basic allure of patterns, how we must constantly toggle between the big picture and the detail, and how the effect of "the whole" can be different from the effect of the individual parts. I explored how our decisionscapes come preloaded with templates that mean we see what we expect to. And I showed how we can introduce new collective templates to help us notice patterns we previously missed. When it comes to tackling the climate crisis, many of our existing mental templates lead us to focus on the wrong thing. For example, when we think of green activities we can do at home, many of us think of recycling—an activity that ranks relatively low on the list of impactful things we can do for the environment. We do not, however, tend to think about our heating systems. This is remarkable as, in the United Kingdom at least, 15 percent of emissions come from domestic heat. To make heating as salient as recycling, we need a new mental model of pollution. Public campaigns can be used to do this. For example, back in the early 2000s, in Australia, the New South Wales Road and Traffic Authority needed to find a way to stop drivers from speeding. Part of the issue was that driving fast was seen as cool by young men. By recasting the behavior, the authorities reasoned, they might be able to stop it. The campaign they landed on showed a young man speeding away from some traffic lights to impress two women. The women, seeing his driving, turn to one another and wiggle their pinkies—a universally understood sign for having a small penis. The ads became instantly iconic, winning awards and criticism in equal measure, and giving pedestrians a new visual language for showing dangerous drivers what they thought of them. Most importantly, though, they completely changed people's perception of speeding, making it embarrassing and emasculating rather than cool and manly. Clearly, we don't want to shame people into adopting heating systems they can't afford, but building a new and highly recognizable archetype of excessive heat consumption could help refocus attention on our highest-emission activities.

In part 4, "The Frame," I showed how the invisible architecture of the environments and systems that surround us shape our perceptions and actions. These forces curtail our decisionscapes, leading us to miss options that fall outside the frame. Our governments' decisionscapes are also curtailed. Political analyst Joseph Overton referred to a "window of discourse"—posthumously dubbed "the Overton window"[2]—limiting the range of policies that the public would find to be politically palatable at a given moment in time. This "window" is the thing the radical flanks I discussed in the last chapter are targeting. When activists with Just Stop Oil throw soup at Van Gogh paintings, they are doing so to force us to notice the frame being imposed. When the Overton window snaps back, those with more moderate views that fall within it suddenly seem more reasonable.

There are other ways that governments blinker their decisionscapes. For example, since most of the day-to-day business of running a country is focused domestically, it may be tempting to immediately look for national solutions to global problems. But, at least when it comes to climate change, this is often not where the highest returns on investment are likely to be. Unlike other environmental issues, such as air pollution, climate change is global rather than local in its impacts. To grossly oversimplify, this means a ton of carbon burned in the United States could affect Nevada and Nairobi equally. Global thinking has been a feature of international climate response, for example, through carbon trading schemes, but not to the extent it should be. Research by Rachel Glennerster and Seema Jayachandran shows how we are falling short.[3] On average, they report, most countries invest 75 percent of their mitigation funds within their own borders. If all emissions were equally easy and equally cost-effective to address, this might make sense, but this is not the reality. Western Europe emits 25 percent more carbon dioxide than South Asia but invests three times as much in mitigation. It isn't just the imbalance that makes this inefficient: the return on investment is often much higher in low- and middle-income countries since the price of avoiding one unit of emissions is much lower in some places than in others. The future returns differ too. The retrofitting needed in most affluent countries costs far more than building green from the outset, and so investments that arrive at the beginning of a period of rapid economic growth can create green path dependency. The message is clear: if our governments looked beyond the domestic frame they have imposed on themselves, their money would do more good for their citizens and for the world.

In writing this book, I hoped the idea of the decisionscape could help make sense of the impossibly complex lives we lead. Being a human has always been difficult. Our sentience often surpasses our ability to bear it, and our intelligence is uncomfortably twinned with the pain that comes from introspection. But in the last hundred years, our lives have become vastly more complicated. The world has collapsed in on itself: we can get anywhere in forty-eight hours, our economies are inextricably linked, and the internet puts us one degree of connection from almost every adult on the planet. This great collapsing has transformed our lives. In the last century, life expectancy has doubled. Today, there are 8 billion people on earth compared to less than 2 billion in 1922. And the technological advances of the last century have been astonishing. These advances have paved the way for seismic social change. A more connected world means, for many, more choice about where to live and work, how to spend our leisure time and money, and everything else we might consider a basic modern freedom. But these new freedoms also come with strings attached; the returns on increased connectivity are diminishing. After all, when our options amplified and became interconnected, so too did the consequences of our actions. As we push deeper into the twenty-first century, the butterfly effects of our consumption are becoming increasingly devastating. Our unsustainable devouring of earth's resources has hurled us into the planet's sixth great extinction, gouged a hole in the ozone layer, and polluted the air we breathe.

We have one chance now to design our way to a better future. If we go against the grain of the decisionscape, we will fail.

Acknowledgments

There are so many people who helped me write this book, in ways big and small.

First, I am grateful for the enthusiastic reaction of my dear friend Kate Glazebrook when I waffled about the germ of this idea back in 2015. Without your generous inquisition, Kate, I would probably never have thought about it with any seriousness. The moment I did return to the idea was during a 10k run in 2019, which my wonderful friend Siân Thurgood was basically hauling me round: sorry, Siân, for slowing the pace even more by huffing my way through a description, and thank you for being fit enough to give me loads of ideas without breaking a sweat!

Thank you to Elizabeth Linos, Lis Costa, and Annie Kirkman for being wonderful thought partners and giving feedback on the framing of the book early on. I am so lucky to have such brilliant minds in my life.

My parents—Sue and Alan Kirkman—read through a draft that only a mother and father could love. They brought new ideas and energy and gave me conviction there was a good enough core to keep working with. Sorry if I challenged the printer, Dad: even from afar I will always end up breaking it!

Hannah Burd deserves eternal appreciation for her detailed read-through, perfectly pitched feedback, and for reminding me that paragraph breaks are not the enemy. The book you read today is far better for Hannah's eagle eye and directness.

Thanks to the Google Docs iPhone app for enabling me to write the start of this mostly in the dead of night while feeding a baby. And thank you to reMarkable for letting me write the rest of this by hand when I hated staring at a computer screen.

I am extremely grateful to the following people for feedback and support: Chris Larkin, whose mind connects unlikely things like no other; Sasha Tregebov, who knows when something that seems boring is interesting and knows when something that seems interesting is boring; Mónica Wills-Silva, whose enthusiasm for the project was contagious just when I really needed to be contaminated; Michael Kaemingk, who has read everything I haven't; Aisling Ní Chonaire, for being a bottomless well of moral support; Ale De Filippo, who pushed me to think about what sketching out a decisionscape would actually look like; Johannes Lohmann, for bravely talking through ideas while we both had ten-week-old babies; Bridget and Pat Gildea for talking this through on a freezing December afternoon with terrible wine and toddlers for company; Catherine Rosales for indulging another presentation from the sofa (it's a weird habit: let's stop!); and Jane Allcock for detailed comments. Thank you also to Stuart Skipp Jr. for answering my random questions about NATO codes and pilot training, and to Stuart Skipp Sr. for suggesting "Why did you buy this book?" as a simple way of helping people understand the idea of the decisionscape.

Without the backing of the MIT Press, this book would not exist. Thank you, Bob Prior, for your support and kindness. Thank you, Matt Browne, for believing in the project and bearing with me while I disappeared to have a baby. I am grateful to Judy Feldmann for painstakingly leading the process of sorting out all my awful grammar and typos and making the book look real. Thank you also to Anne-Marie Bono, who always seems to have the answers to my panicked questions driven entirely by my own disorganization. And thank you to the peer reviewers whose names I do not know! Your suggestions helped me find the dropped stitches at the end of this project.

Finally, thank you to my wonderful wife, Mel, who gave me the most useful help of all: time to myself to work on this when I really needed it. And to my girls, Imogen and Evie, for the ultimate meta-contribution: giving me perspective.

Notes

CHAPTER 1

1. Adam Brumm, Adhi Agus Oktaviana, Basran Burhan, Budianto Hakim, Rustan Lebe, Jian-xin Zhao, Priyatno Hadi Sulistyarto et al., "Oldest Cave Art Found in Sulawesi," *Science Advances* 7, no. 3 (2021): eabd4648.

2. Gábor Jandó, Eszter Mikó-Baráth, Katalin Markó, Katalin Hollódy, Béla Török, and Ilona Kovacs, "Early-Onset Binocularity in Preterm Infants Reveals Experience-Dependent Visual Development in Humans," *Proceedings of the National Academy of Sciences* 109, no. 27 (2012): 11049–11052.

3. Martin J. Doherty, Nicola M. Campbell, Hiromi Tsuji, and William A. Phillips, "The Ebbinghaus Illusion Deceives Adults but Not Young Children," *Developmental Science* 13, no. 5 (2010): 714–721.

4. Mario Ponzo, *Intorno ad alcune illusioni nel campo delle sensazioni tattili, sull'illusione di Aristotele e fenomeni analoghi* (Wilhelm Engelmann, 1910).

5. H. Leibowitz, R. Brislin, L. Perlmutrer, and R. Hennessy, "Ponzo Perspective Illusion as a Manifestation of Space Perception," *Science* 166, no. 3909 (1969): 1174–1176.

6. Herschel W. Leibowitz and Herbert A. Pick, "Cross-Cultural and Educational Aspects of the Ponzo Perspective Illusion," *Perception & Psychophysics* 12, no. 5 (1972): 430–432.

7. Samy Rima, Carla Khalil, Benoit R. Cottereau, Yves Trotter, and Jean-Baptiste Durand, "Asymmetry of Pictorial Space: A Cultural Phenomenon," *Journal of Vision* 19, no. 4 (2019): 22.

CHAPTER 2

1. Keith Marzilli Ericson and David Laibson, "Intertemporal Choice," in *Handbook of Behavioral Economics: Applications and Foundations*, vol. 2, ed. B. Douglas Bernheim, Stefano DellaVigna, and David Laibson (Amsterdam: North-Holland, 2019), 1–67.

2. Rebecca Ponce de Leon, Jacqueline R. Rifkin, and Richard P. Larrick, "'They're Everywhere!': Symbolically Threatening Groups Seem More Pervasive Than Nonthreatening Groups," *Psychological Science* (2022): 09567976211060009.

3. Jay J. Van Bavel and William A. Cunningham, "A Social Identity Approach to Person Memory: Group Membership, Collective Identification, and Social Role Shape Attention and Memory," *Personality and Social Psychology Bulletin* 38, no. 12 (2012): 1566–1578.

4. Y. Jenny Xiao and Jay J. Van Bavel, "See Your Friends Close and Your Enemies Closer: Social Identity and Identity Threat Shape the Representation of Physical Distance," *Personality and Social Psychology Bulletin* 38, no. 7 (2012): 959–972.

5. Amos Tversky and Daniel Kahneman, "Availability: A Heuristic for Judging Frequency and Probability," *Cognitive Psychology* 5, no. 2 (1973): 207–232.

6. "Risk of Death: 18 Things More Likely to Kill You Than Sharks," Florida Museum, accessed July 19, 2022, https://www.floridamuseum.ufl.edu/shark-attacks/odds/compare-risk/death.

7. Yaacov Trope and Nira Liberman, "Construal-Level Theory of Psychological Distance," *Psychological Review* 117, no. 2 (2010): 440.

8. Lee Ross, "From the Fundamental Attribution Error to the Truly Fundamental Attribution Error and Beyond: My Research Journey," *Perspectives on Psychological Science* 13, no. 6 (2018): 750–769.

9. Roy Frink Street, "A Gestalt Completion Test," *Teachers College Contributions to Education* (1931).

10. Jens Förster, Ronald S. Friedman, and Nira Liberman, "Temporal Construal Effects on Abstract and Concrete Thinking: Consequences for Insight and Creative Cognition," *Journal of Personality and Social Psychology* 87, no. 2 (2004): 177.

11. Kwo Da-Wei, *Chinese Brushwork in Calligraphy and Painting: Its History, Aesthetics, and Techniques* (North Chelmsford, MA: Courier Corporation, 2012).

12. Victoria Rodway, Bethany Tatham, and Kun Guo, "Effect of Model Race and Viewing Perspective on Body Attractiveness and Body Size Assessment in Young Caucasian Women: An Eye-Tracking Study," *Psychological Research* 83, no. 2 (2019): 347–356.

13. N. Schneider, K. Frieler, E. Pfeiffer, U. Lehmkuhl, and Salbach-Andrae, H., 2009, "Comparison of Body Size Estimation in Adolescents with Different Types of Eating Disorders," *European Eating Disorders Review: The Professional Journal of the Eating Disorders Association* 17, no. 6 (2009): 468–475.

14. Richard H. Thaler and Cass R. Sunstein, *Nudge: Improving Decisions about Health, Wealth, and Happiness* (New York: Penguin, 2009).

15. Ruth Schmidt, "A Model for Choice Infrastructure: Looking beyond Choice Architecture in Behavioral Public Policy," *Behavioural Public Policy* (2022): 1–26.

16. Yoav Bar-Anan, Nira Liberman, Yaacov Trope, and Daniel Algom, "Automatic Processing of Psychological Distance: Evidence from a Stroop Task," *Journal of Experimental Psychology: General* 136, no. 4 (2007): 610.

CHAPTER 3

1. Roger Fisher, "Preventing Nuclear War," *Bulletin of the Atomic Scientists* 37, no. 3 (1981): 11–17.

2. Philippa Foot, "The Problem of Abortion and the Doctrine of the Double Effect," *Oxford Review* 5 (1967).

3. Joshua D. Greene, "Beyond Point-and-Shoot Morality: Why Cognitive (Neuro) Science Matters for Ethics," *Ethics* 124, no. 4 (2014): 695–726.

4. Hong Im Shin and Juyoung Kim, "Foreign Language Effect and Psychological Distance," *Journal of Psycholinguistic Research* 46, no. 6 (2017): 1339–1352.

5. "The Secret Death Toll of Amercia's Drones," *New York Times*, March 30, 2019, https://www.nytimes.com/2019/03/30/opinion/drones-civilian-casulaties-trump-obama.html.

6. Christoph Engel, "Dictator Games: A Meta Study," *Experimental Economics* 14, no. 4 (2011): 583–610.

7. Justin Cheng, Michael Bernstein, Cristian Danescu-Niculescu-Mizil, and Jure Leskovec, "Anyone Can Become a Troll: Causes of Trolling Behavior in Online Discussions," in *Proceedings of the 2017 ACM Conference on Computer Supported Cooperative Work and Social Computing* (New York: Association for Computing Machinery, 2017), 1217–1230.

8. Jeremy Prichard, Richard Wortley, Paul A. Watters, Caroline Spiranovic, Charlotte Hunn, and Tony Krone, "Effects of Automated Messages on Internet Users Attempting to Access 'Barely Legal' Pornography," *Sexual Abuse* 34, no. 1 (2022): 106–124.

9. Edmond Awad, Sohan Dsouza, Richard Kim, Jonathan Schulz, Joseph Henrich, Azim Shariff, Jean-François Bonnefon, and Iyad Rahwan, "The Moral Machine Experiment," *Nature* 563, no. 7729 (2018): 59–64.

10. Prichard et al., "Effects of Automated Messages on Internet Users."

11. Peter Singer, *Famine, Affluence, and Morality* (New York: Oxford University Press, 2016).

12. George Eliot, *Middlemarch* (1871; Modern Library, 2000).

13. Sam Corbett-Davies, Pierson, Emma, Feller, Avi, and Sharad Goel, "A Computer Program Used for Bail and Sentencing Decisions Was Labeled Biased against Blacks. It's Actually Not That Clear," *Washington Post,* October 17, 2016, https://www.washingtonpost.com/news/monkey-cage/wp/2016/10/17/can-an-algorithm-be-racist-our-analysis-is-more-cautious-than-propublicas.

CHAPTER 4

1. Ann E. Tenbrunsel and David M. Messick, "Ethical Fading: The Role of Self-Deception in Unethical Behavior," *Social Justice Research* 17 (2004): 223–236.

2. Herbert A. Simon, "Bounded Rationality," in *Utility and Probability*, edited by John Eatwell, Murray Milgate, and Peter Newman (New York: Palgrave Macmillan, 1990), 15–18.

3. Dolly Chugh, Max H. Bazerman, and Mahzarin R. Banaji, "Bounded Ethicality as a Psychological Barrier to Recognizing Conflicts of Interest," in

Conflicts of Interest: Challenges and Solutions in Business, Law, Medicine, and Public Policy, edited by Don A. Moore, Daylian M. Cain, George Loewenstein, and Max H. Bazerman (Cambridge: Cambridge University Press, 2005), 74–95.

4. Ting Zhang, Pinar O. Fletcher, Francesca Gino, and Max H. Bazerman, "Reducing Bounded Ethicality: How to Help Individuals Notice and Avoid Unethical Behavior," *Organizational Dynamics* 44, no. 4 (2015): 310–317.

5. Susan S. Woodhouse, Julie R. Scott, Allison D. Hepworth, and Jude Cassidy, "Secure Base Provision: A New Approach to Examining Links between Maternal Caregiving and Infant Attachment," *Child Development* 91, no. 1 (2020): e249–e265.

6. Atul Guwande, *The Checklist Manifesto: How to Get Things Right* (New York: Picador, 2010).

7. Michael Hallsworth, Tim Chadborn, Anna Sallis, Michael Sanders, Daniel Berry, Felix Greaves, Lara Clements, and Sally C. Davies, "Provision of Social Norm Feedback to High Prescribers of Antibiotics in General Practice: A Pragmatic National Randomised Controlled Trial," *The Lancet* 387, no. 10029 (2016): 1743–1752.

8. Beth Veinott, Gary A. Klein, and Sterling Wiggins, "Evaluating the Effectiveness of the Premortem Technique on Plan Confidence," in *ISCRAM 2010—7th International Conference on Information Systems for Crisis Response and Management: Defining Crisis Management 3.0, Proceedings*, edited by C. Zobel and B. T. S. French (Seattle: Information Systems for Crisis Response and Management, 2010).

CHAPTER 5

1. Robert Stickgold, April Malia, Denise Maguire, David Roddenberry, and Margaret O'Connor, "Replaying the Game: Hypnagogic Images in Normals and Amnesics," *Science* 290, no. 5490 (2000): 350–353.

2. *International Classification of Diseases Eleventh Revision (ICD-11)* (Geneva: World Health Organization, 2019).

3. Elizabeth Linos, Krista Ruffini, and Stephanie Wilcoxen, "Reducing Burnout and Resignations among Frontline Workers: A Field Experiment,"

Journal of Public Administration Research and Theory 32, no. 3 (2022): 473–488.

4.   Adam M. Grant and David A. Hofmann, "Outsourcing Inspiration: The Performance Effects of Ideological Messages from Leaders and Beneficiaries," *Organizational Behavior and Human Decision Processes* 116, no. 2 (2011): 173–187.

5.   Nicola Bellé, "Experimental Evidence on the Relationship between Public Service Motivation and Job Performance," *Public Administration Review* (2013): 143–153.

6.   Karl Duncker and Lynne S. Lees, "On Problem-Solving," *Psychological Monographs* 58, no. 5 (1945): i.

7.   Tony McCaffrey, "Innovation Relies on the Obscure: A Key to Overcoming the Classic Problem of Functional Fixedness," *Psychological Science* 23, no. 3 (2012): 215–218.

CHAPTER 6

1.   Derek Parfit, *On What Matters,* 2 vols. (Oxford: Oxford University Press, 2011).

2.   Philip G. Zimbardo and John N. Boyd, "Putting Time in Perspective: A Valid, Reliable Individual-Differences Metric," in *Time Perspective Theory: Review, Research and Application*, edited by Maciej Stolarski, Nicolas Fieulaine, and Wessel van Beekpp (Cham: Springer, 2015), 17–55.

3.   Maciej Stolarski, Marcin Zajenkowski, Konrad S. Jankowski, and Kinga Szymaniak, "Deviation from the Balanced Time Perspective: A Systematic Review of Empirical Relationships with Psychological Variables," *Personality and Individual Differences* 156 (2020): 109772.

4.   John N. Boyd and Philip G. Zimbardo, "Constructing Time after Death: The Transcendental-Future Time Perspective," *Time & Society* 6, no. 1 (1997): 35–54.

5.   Philip Zimbardo and John Boyd, *The Time Paradox: The New Psychology of Time That Will Change Your Life.* (New York: Simon and Schuster, 2008); John Boyd, "The Marshmallow Game: Modifying Kid's Time Perspective," *The Time Paradox*, accessed December 18, 2022, https://www.thetime paradox.com/2008/09/02/the-marshmallow-game-modifying-kids-time -perspective.

6. Susan E. Mayer, Ariel Kalil, Philip Oreopoulos, and Sebastian Gallegos, "Using Behavioral Insights to Increase Parental Engagement: The Parents and Children Together Intervention," *Journal of Human Resources* 54, no. 4 (2019): 900–925.

7. Oliver P. Hauser, David G. Rand, Alexander Peysakhovich, and Martin A. Nowak, "Cooperating with the Future," *Nature* 511, no. 7508 (2014): 220–223.

8. Jeffrey B. Liebman and Neale Mahoney, "Do Expiring Budgets Lead to Wasteful Year-End Spending? Evidence from Federal Procurement," *American Economic Review* 107, no. 11 (2017): 3510–3549.

CHAPTER 7

1. Mihaly Csikszentmihalyi, *Flow* (Cophenagen: Munksgaard, 1991).

2. Ceri Evans, *Perform Under Pressure* (New York: HarperCollins, 2019).

3. Dolly Chugh and Max H. Bazerman, "Bounded Awareness: What You Fail to See Can Hurt You," *Mind & Society* 6 (2007): 1–18.

4. Richard Nisbett, *The Geography of Thought: How Asians and Westerners Think Differently . . . and Why* (New York: Simon and Schuster, 2004).

5. Erich Fromm, *The Art of Loving: The Centennial Edition* (London: A&C Black, 2000).

6. Julianne Holt-Lunstad, Timothy B. Smith, and J. Bradley Layton, "Social Relationships and Mortality Risk: A Meta-Analytic Review," *PLOS Medicine* 7, no. 7 (2010): e1000316.

7. Bokyung Kim, Young Shin Sung, and Samuel M. McClure, "The Neural Basis of Cultural Differences in Delay Discounting," *Philosophical Transactions of the Royal Society B: Biological Sciences* 367, no. 1589 (2012): 650–656.

8. Ting Kin Ng and Daniel Fu Keung Wong, "The Efficacy of Cognitive Behavioral Therapy for Chinese People: A Meta-Analysis," *Australian & New Zealand Journal of Psychiatry* 52, no. 7 (2018): 620–637.

9. Marcus E. Raichle, Ann Mary MacLeod, Abraham Z. Snyder, William J. Powers, Debra A. Gusnard, and Gordon L. Shulman, "A Default Mode of Brain Function," *Proceedings of the National Academy of Sciences* 98, no. 2 (2001): 676–682.

10. Li Zhang, Tiangang Zhou, Jian Zhang, Zuxiang Liu, Jin Fan, and Ying Zhu, "In Search of the Chinese Self: An fMRI Study," *Science in China Series C* 49, no. 1 (2006): 89–96.

11. Robin L. Carhart-Harris, Suresh Muthukumaraswamy, Leor Roseman, Mendel Kaelen, Wouter Droog, Kevin Murphy, Enzo Tagliazucchi et al., "Neural Correlates of the LSD Experience Revealed by Multimodal Neuro-imaging," *Proceedings of the National Academy of Sciences* 113, no. 17 (2016): 4853–4858.

12. Albert Hofmann, *LSD: My Problem Child* (Oxford: Oxford University Press, 2013).

13. Bruno Romeo, Laurent Karila, Catherine Martelli, and Amine Benyamina, "Efficacy of Psychedelic Treatments on Depressive Symptoms: A Meta-Analysis," *Journal of Psychopharmacology* 34, no. 10 (2020): 1079–1085.

14. James J. Gattuso, Daniel Perkins, Simon Ruffell, Andrew J. Lawrence, Daniel Hoyer, Laura H. Jacobson, Christopher Timmermann et al., "Default Mode Network Modulation by Psychedelics: A Systematic Review," *International Journal of Neuropsychopharmacology* 26, no. 3 (2023): 155–188.

15. James W. Pennebaker, "The Secret Life of Pronouns," *New Scientist* 211, no. 2828 (2011): 42–45.

16. James W. Pennebaker and Cindy K. Chung, "Expressive Writing, Emotional Upheavals, and Health," *Foundations of Health Psychology*, edited by Howard S. Friedman and Roxane Cohen Silver (Oxford: Oxford University Press, 2007), 263–284.

17. Michael Sanders, Guglielmo Briscese, Rory Gallagher, Alex Gyani, Samuel Hanes, and Elspeth Kirkman, "Behavioural Insight and the Labour Market: Evidence from a Pilot Study and a Large Stepped-Wedge Controlled Trial," *Journal of Public Policy* 41, no. 1 (2021): 42–65.

CHAPTER 8

1. John Rawls, *A Theory of Justice* (Cambridge, MA: Belknap, 1971).

2. Karen Huang, Joshua D. Greene, and Max Bazerman, "Veil-of-Ignorance Reasoning Favors the Greater Good," *Proceedings of the National Academy of Sciences* 116, no. 48 (2019): 23989–23995.

3. Venoo Kakar, Julisa Franco, Joel Voelz, and Julia Wu, "Effects of Host Race Information on Airbnb Listing Prices in San Francisco," MPRA Paper 69974, University Library of Munich, Germany (2016); Benjamin Edelman, Michael Luca, and Dan Svirsky, "Racial Discrimination in the Sharing Economy: Evidence from a Field Experiment," *American Economic Journal: Applied Economics* 9, no. 2 (2017): 1–22.

4. Marianne Bertrand and Sendhil Mullainathan, "Are Emily and Greg More Employable Than Lakisha and Jamal? A Field Experiment on Labor Market Discrimination," *American Economic Review* 94, no. 4 (2004): 991–1013.

5. Zack Adesina and Oana Marocico, "Is It Easier to Get a Job if You're Adam or Mohamed?" *BBC News*, February 6, 2017, https://www.bbc.co.uk/news/uk-england-london-38751307.

6. Magnus Carlsson, Henning Finseraas, Arnfinn H. Midtbøen, and Guðbjörg Linda Rafnsdóttir, "Gender Bias in Academic Recruitment? Evidence from a Survey Experiment in the Nordic Region," *European Sociological Review* 37, no. 3 (2021): 399–410.

7. Kate Glazebrook, "Can We Predict Applicant Performance without Requiring CVs?—Putting Applied to the Test [Part 1]," *Applied.com,* September 21, 2016, https://www.beapplied.com/post/can-we-predict-applicant-performance-without-requiring-cvs-putting-applied-to-the-test-part-1.

8. Florian Foos and Daniel Bischof, "Tabloid Media Campaigns and Public Opinion: Quasi-Experimental Evidence on Euroscepticism in England," *American Political Science Review* 116, no. 1 (2022): 19–37.

9. David Broockman and Joshua Kalla, "The Impacts of Selective Partisan Media Exposure: A Field Experiment with Fox News Viewers," *OSF Preprints* 1 (2022).

10. Peter Schwardmann, Egon Tripodi, and Joël J. Van der Weele, "Self-Persuasion: Evidence from Field Experiments at International Debating Competitions," *American Economic Review* 112, no. 4 (2022): 1118–1146.

11. Hunter Gehlbach, Maureen E. Brinkworth, Aaron M. King, Laura M. Hsu, Joseph McIntyre, and Todd Rogers, "Creating Birds of Similar Feathers: Leveraging Similarity to Improve Teacher–Student Relationships and Academic Achievement," *Journal of Educational Psychology* 108, no. 3 (2016): 342.

12. Elspeth Kirkman, "Free Riding or Discounted Riding? How the Framing of a Bike Share Offer Impacts Offer-Redemption," *Journal of Behavioral Public Administration* 2, no. 2 (2019).

CHAPTER 9

1. Jacob R. Brown, Ryan D. Enos, James Feigenbaum, and Soumyajit Mazumder, "Childhood Cross-Ethnic Exposure Predicts Political Behavior Seven Decades Later: Evidence from Linked Administrative Data," *Science Advances* 7, no. 24 (2021): eabe8432.

2. Raj Chetty, Nathaniel Hendren, and Lawrence F. Katz, "The Effects of Exposure to Better Neighborhoods on Children: New Evidence from the Moving to Opportunity Experiment," *American Economic Review* 106, no. 4 (2016): 855–902.

3. Michael Hallsworth, John A. List, Robert D. Metcalfe, and Ivo Vlaev, "The Behavioralist as Tax Collector: Using Natural Field Experiments to Enhance Tax Compliance," *Journal of Public Economics* 148 (2017): 14–31.

4. Hunt Allcott, "Social Norms and Energy Conservation," *Journal of Public Economics* 95, nos. 9–10 (2011): 1082–1095.

5. Margaret E. Tankard and Elizabeth Levy Paluck, "The Effect of a Supreme Court Decision Regarding Gay Marriage on Social Norms and Personal Attitudes," *Psychological Science* 28, no. 9 (2017): 1334–1344.

6. Christine M. Schroeder and Deborah A. Prentice, "Exposing Pluralistic Ignorance to Reduce Alcohol Use among College Students 1," *Journal of Applied Social Psychology* 28, no. 23 (1998): 2150–2180.

7. Leonardo Bursztyn, Alessandra L. González, and David Yanagizawa-Drott, "Misperceived Social Norms: Women Working Outside the Home in Saudi Arabia," *American Economic Review* 110, no. 10 (2020): 2997–3029.

8. Mary Oliver, "The Summer Day," *New and Selected Poems* 1 (1992).

9. Juliana Schroeder and Nicholas Epley, "Demeaning: Dehumanizing Others by Minimizing the Importance of Their Psychological Needs," *Journal of Personality and Social Psychology* 119, no. 4 (2020): 765.

10. Social Mobility Commission, "Elitist Britain 2019—The Educational Backgrounds of Britain's Leading People" (2019), https://www.gov.uk

/government/publications/elitist-britain-2019/elitist-britain-2019-the
-educational-backgrounds-of-britains-leading-people.

11. Elizabeth Levy Paluck, Hana Shepherd, and Peter M. Aronow, "Changing Climates of Conflict: A Social Network Experiment in 56 Schools," *Proceedings of the National Academy of Sciences* 113, no. 3 (2016): 566–571.

12. Michael Bernstein and Emily Ekins, "Are Ideological Differences the Only Reason Republicans and Democrats Can't Agree?" *CATO Institute*, October 27, 2020, https://www.cato.org/blog/are-ideological-differences-only -reason-republicans-democrats-cant-agree.

CHAPTER 10

1. Alison Wood Brooks, "Get Excited: Reappraising Pre-Performance Anxiety as Excitement," *Journal of Experimental Psychology: General* 143, no. 3 (2014): 1144.

2. George F. Loewenstein, Elke U. Weber, Christopher K. Hsee, and Ned Welch, "Risk as Feelings," *Psychological Bulletin* 127, no. 2 (2001): 267.

3. Daniel Kahneman, *Thinking, Fast and Slow* (New York: Macmillan, 2011).

4. Bruce Ian Carlin and David T. Robinson, *Fear and Loathing in Las Vegas: Evidence from Blackjack Tables* (National Bureau of Economic Research, 2009).

5. Kristi D. Wright, Megan A. N. Adams Lebell, and R. Nicholas Carleton, "Intolerance of Uncertainty, Anxiety Sensitivity, Health Anxiety, and Anxiety Disorder Symptoms in Youth," *Journal of Anxiety Disorders* 41 (2016): 35–42.

6. Annie Duke, *Thinking in Bets: Making Smarter Decisions When You Don't Have All the Facts* (New York: Penguin, 2019).

7. Amos Tversky and Daniel Kahneman, "Availability: A Heuristic for Judging Frequency and Probability," *Cognitive Psychology* 5, no. 2 (1973): 207–232.

8. Blalock Garrick, Vrinda Kadiyali, and Daniel H. Simon, "Driving Fatalities after 9/11: A Hidden Cost of Terrorism," *Applied Economics* 41, no. 14 (2009): 1717–1729.

9. G. M. Casey, B. Burnell, M. Morris, A. Parberry, N. Singh, and A. Rosenthal, "Celebrities and Screening: A Measurable Impact on High-Grade

Cervical Neoplasia Diagnosis from the 'Jade Goody Effect' in the UK," *British Journal of Cancer* 109, no. 5 (2013): 1192–1197.

10. Conor Stewart, "MDMA Related Drug Deaths England & Wales 2021," *Statista*, November 3, 2022, https://www.statista.com/statistics/470824/drug-poisoning-deaths-mdma-ecstasy-in-england-and-wales.

11. Dominik Mischkowski, Ethan Kross, and Brad J. Bushman, "Flies on the Wall Are Less Aggressive: Self-Distancing 'in the Heat of the Moment' Reduces Aggressive Thoughts, Angry Feelings and Aggressive Behavior," *Journal of Experimental Social Psychology* 48, no. 5 (2012): 1187–1191.

12. Shayna Skakoon-Sparling, Kenneth M. Cramer, and Paul A. Shuper, "The Impact of Sexual Arousal on Sexual Risk-Taking and Decision-Making in Men and Women," *Archives of Sexual Behavior* 45 (2016): 33–42.

PART III

1. A. N. Whitehead and Lucien Price, *Dialogues of Alfred North Whitehead* (1954; Boston: David Godine, 2001).

CHAPTER 11

1. Katherine Clayton, "Sophia David '21 Featured in Science News for Students," *Friends' Central School*, May 12, 2021, https://www.friendscentral.org/news/news-posts-direct-links/~board/homepage/post/sophia-david-21-featured-in-science-news-for-students.

2. Salvador Dalí, *The Secret Life of Salvador Dalí,* trans. Haakon M. Chevalier (New York: Dial, 1942), 3.

3. Tim Newark, *The Book of Camouflage: The Art of Disappearing* (New York: Bloomsbury, 2013).

4. David Navon, "Forest Before Trees: The Precedence of Global Features in Visual Perception," *Cognitive Psychology* 9, no. 3 (1977): 353–383.

5. Wen Wen and Hideaki Kawabata, "Impact of Navon-Induced Global and Local Processing Biases on the Acquisition of Spatial Knowledge," *SAGE Open* 8, no. 2 (2018): 2158244018769131.

6. C. Neil Macrae and Helen L. Lewis, "Do I Know You? Processing Orientation and Face Recognition," *Psychological Science* 13, no. 2 (2002): 194–196.

7. Edith Fischer and Richard F. Haines, *Cognitive Issues in Head-Up Displays*, NASA Technical Paper 1711 (NASA, 1980).

8. Benjamin J. Dixon, Michael J. Daly, Harley HL Chan, Allan Vescan, Ian J. Witterick, and Jonathan C. Irish, "Inattentional Blindness Increased with Augmented Reality Surgical Navigation," *American Journal of Rhinology & Allergy* 28, no. 5 (2014): 433–437.

9. Jessica Wapner, "Vision and Breathing May Be the Secrets to Surviving 2020," *Scientific American*, November 16, 2020, https://www.scientific american.com/article/vision-and-breathing-may-be-the-secrets-to-surviving -2020.

10. Ira E. Hyman Jr., Benjamin A. Sarb, and Breanne M. Wise-Swanson, "Failure to See Money on a Tree: Inattentional Blindness for Objects That Guided Behavior," *Frontiers in Psychology* 5 (2014): 356; Ira E. Hyman Jr., S. Matthew Boss, Breanne M. Wise, Kira E. McKenzie, and Jenna M. Caggiano, "Did You See the Unicycling Clown? Inattentional Blindness while Walking and Talking on a Cell Phone," *Applied Cognitive Psychology* 24, no. 5 (2010): 597–607.

11. Daniel J. Simons and Michael D. Schlosser, "Inattentional Blindness for a Gun During a Simulated Police Vehicle Stop," *Cognitive Research: Principles and Implications* 2, no. 1 (2017): 1–8; Alia N. Wulff and Ira E. Hyman Jr., "Crime Blindness: The Impact of Inattentional Blindness on Eyewitness Awareness, Memory, and Identification," *Applied Cognitive Psychology* 36, no. 1 (2022): 166–178; Jiayu Chen, Xinyi Song, and Zhenghang Lin, "Revealing the 'Invisible Gorilla' in Construction: Estimating Construction Safety through Mental Workload Assessment," *Automation in Construction* 63 (2016): 173–183.

12. Daniel J. Simons and Christopher F. Chabris, "Gorillas in Our Midst: Sustained Inattentional Blindness for Dynamic Events," *Perception* 28, no. 9 (1999): 1059–1074.

13. Trafton Drew, Melissa L-H. Võ, and Jeremy M. Wolfe, "The Invisible Gorilla Strikes Again: Sustained Inattentional Blindness in Expert Observers," *Psychological Science* 24, no. 9 (2013): 1848–1853.

14. Henry L. Roediger and Kathleen B. McDermott, "Creating False Memories: Remembering Words Not Presented in Lists," *Journal of Experimental Psychology: Learning, Memory, and Cognition* 21, no. 4 (1995): 803.

15. "Understanding QAnon's Connection to American Politics, Religion, and Media Consumption," *PRRI*, May 27, 2021, https://www.prri.org/research /qanon-conspiracy-american-politics-report.

16. Alex Bellos, *Alex through the Looking-Glass: How Life Reflects Numbers, and Numbers Reflect Life* (London: A&C Black, 2014).

17. Marc-André Schulz, Barbara Schmalbach, Peter Brugger, and Karsten Witt, "Analysing Humanly Generated Random Number Sequences: A Pattern-Based Approach," *PLOS ONE* 7, no. 7 (2012): e41531.

18. Joseph Henrich, *The Secret of Our Success: How Culture Is Driving Human Evolution, Domesticating Our Species, and Making Us Smarter* (Princeton, NJ: Princeton University Press, 2015).

19. Alison Gopnik, Thomas L. Griffiths, and Christopher G. Lucas, "When Younger Learners Can Be Better (or at Least More Open-Minded) Than Older Ones," *Current Directions in Psychological Science* 24, no. 2 (2015): 87–92.

CHAPTER 12

1. IFPI, *Music Consumer Insight Report 2018* (London: IFPI, 2018), https:// www.ifpi.org/wp-content/uploads/2020/07/091018_Music-Consumer -Insight-Report-2018.pdf.

2. "Meta Counterfeit and Piracy Campaign," *Gov.uk*, December 19, 2022, https://www.gov.uk/government/publications/meta-counterfeit-and-piracy -campaign.

3. Gilles Grolleau and Luc Meunier, "Doing More with Less: Behavioral Insights for Anti-Piracy Messages," *Information Society* 38, no. 5 (2022): 388–393.

4. Michelle R. Kaufman, Alyssa Mooney, Benjamin Kamala, Najmeh Modarres, Robert Karam, and Deo Ng'Wanansabi, "Effects of the Fataki Campaign: Addressing Cross-Generational Sex in Tanzania by Mobilizing Communities to Intervene," *AIDS and Behavior* 17, no. 6 (2013): 2053–2062.

5. Kevin M. Swartout, Mary P. Koss, Jacquelyn W. White, Martie P. Thompson, Antonia Abbey, and Alexandra L. Bellis, "Trajectory Analysis of the Campus Serial Rapist Assumption," *JAMA Pediatrics* 169, no. 12 (2015): 1148–1154.

6.   George Lakoff, *Fire, Women, and Dangerous Things: What Categories Reveal about the Mind* (Chicago: University of Chicago Press, 1987).

7.   Christian Dahlman, Farhan Sarwar, Rasmus Bååth, Lena Wahlberg, and Sverker Sikström, "Prototype Effect and the Persuasiveness of Generalizations," *Review of Philosophy and Psychology* 7, no. 1 (2016): 163–180.

CHAPTER 13

1.   William E. Gladstone, *Studies on Homer and the Homeric Age* (1853; Cambridge: Cambridge University Press, 2010).

2.   Brent Berlin and Paul Kay, *Basic Color Terms: Their Universality and Evolution* (1969; Berkeley: University of California Press, 1991).

3.   Kenny Coventry, Christos Mitsakis, Ian Davies, Julio Lillo Jover, Anna Androulaki, and Natalia Gômez-Pestaña, "Basic Colour Terms in Modern Greek: Twelve Terms Including Two Blues," *Journal of Greek Linguistics* 7, no. 1 (2006): 3–47.

4.   Debi Roberson, Ian Davies, and Jules Davidoff, "Color Categories Are Not Universal: Replications and New Evidence from a Stone-Age Culture," *Journal of Experimental Psychology: General* 129, no. 3 (2000): 369.

5.   Panos Athanasopoulos, "Cognitive Representation of Colour in Bilinguals: The Case of Greek Blues," *Bilingualism: Language and Cognition* 12, no. 1 (2009): 83–95.

6.   Nick J. Enfield, Asifa Majid, and Miriam Van Staden, "Cross-Linguistic Categorisation of the Body: Introduction," *Language Sciences* 28, no. 2–3 (2006): 137–147.

7.   Tatiana Sokolova, Satheesh Seenivasan, and Manoj Thomas, "The Left-Digit Bias: When and Why Are Consumers Penny Wise and Pound Foolish?," *Journal of Marketing Research* 57, no. 4 (2020): 771–788.

8.   Matthew Lee, Arzi Adbi, and Jasjit Singh, "Categorical Cognition and Outcome Efficiency in Impact Investing Decisions," *Strategic Management Journal* 41, no. 1 (2020): 86–107.

9.   Jennifer L. Doleac and Luke C. D. Stein, "The Visible Hand: Race and Online Market Outcomes," *Economic Journal* 123, no. 572 (2013): F469–F492.

10. Evan P. Apfelbaum, Samuel R. Sommers, and Michael I. Norton, "Seeing Race and Seeming Racist? Evaluating Strategic Colorblindness in Social Interaction," *Journal of Personality and Social Psychology* 95, no. 4 (2008): 918.

11. Evan P. Apfelbaum, Kristin Pauker, Nalini Ambady, Samuel R. Sommers, and Michael I. Norton, "Learning (Not) to Talk about Race: When Older Children Underperform in Social Categorization," *Developmental Psychology* 44, no. 5 (2008): 1513.

12. Neda Maghbouleh, Ariela Schachter, and René D. Flores, "Middle Eastern and North African Americans May Not Be Perceived, Nor Perceive Themselves, to Be White," *Proceedings of the National Academy of Sciences* 119, no. 7 (2022): e2117940119.

13. Nadia N. Abuelezam, Abdulrahman M. El-Sayed, and Sandro Galea, "The Health of Arab Americans in the United States: An Updated Comprehensive Literature Review," *Frontiers in Public Health* 6 (2018): 262.

CHAPTER 14

1. Emile Durkheim, *The Elementary Forms of the Religious Life: The Totemic System in Australia* (Paris: Alcan, 1912).

2. Dimitris Xygalatas, Ivana Konvalinka, Joseph Bulbulia, and Andreas Roepstorff, "Quantifying Collective Effervescence: Heart-Rate Dynamics at a Fire-Walking Ritual," *Communicative & Integrative Biology* 4, no. 6 (2011): 735–738.

3. G. Baranowski-Pinto, V. L. S. Profeta, Martha Newson, H. Whitehouse, and D. Xygalatas, "Being in a Crowd Bonds People via Physiological Synchrony," *Scientific Reports* 12, no. 1 (2022): 1–10.

4. Zhongqiang Sun, Wenjun Yu, Jifan Zhou, and Mowei Shen, "Perceiving Crowd Attention: Gaze Following in Human Crowds with Conflicting Cues," *Attention, Perception, & Psychophysics* 79, no. 4 (2017): 1039–1049.

5. Yi Ma, Eric Wai Ming Lee, Meng Shi, and Richard Kwok Kit Yuen, "Spontaneous Synchronization of Motion in Pedestrian Crowds of Different Densities," *Nature Human Behaviour* 5, no. 4 (2021): 447–457.

6. Steven H. Strogatz, Daniel M. Abrams, Allan McRobie, Bruno Eckhardt, and Edward Ott, "Crowd Synchrony on the Millennium Bridge," *Nature* 438, no. 7064 (2005): 43–44.

7. Serguei Saavedra, Kathleen Hagerty, and Brian Uzzi, "Synchronicity, Instant Messaging, and Performance among Financial Traders," *Proceedings of the National Academy of Sciences* 108, no. 13 (2011): 5296–5301.

8. Renee Timmers, Satoshi Endo, Adrian Bradbury, and Alan M. Wing, "Synchronization and Leadership in String Quartet Performance: A Case Study of Auditory and Visual Cues," *Frontiers in Psychology* 5 (2014): 645.

9. Damon Centola, *How Behavior Spreads: The Science of Complex Contagions*, vol. 3 (Princeton, NJ: Princeton University Press, 2018).

PART IV

1. Jacques Derrida, *Monolingualism of the Other, or The Prosthesis of Origin*, trans. Patrick Mensah (Stanford, CA: Stanford University Press, 1998).

CHAPTER 15

1. Roger Neustadter, "Beat the Clock: The Mid-20th-Century Protest against the Reification of Time," *Time & Society* 1, no. 3 (1992): 379–398.

2. Eric J. Allen, Patricia M. Dechow, Devin G. Pope, and George Wu, "Reference-Dependent Preferences: Evidence from Marathon Runners," *Management Science* 63, no. 6 (2017): 1657–1672.

3. Meng Zhu, Rajesh Bagchi, and Stefan J. Hock, "The Mere Deadline Effect: Why More Time Might Sabotage Goal Pursuit," *Journal of Consumer Research* 45, no. 5 (2019): 1068–1084.

4. Ajay Kalra, Xiao Liu, and Wei Zhang, "The Zero Bias in Target Retirement Fund Choice," *Journal of Consumer Research* 47, no. 4 (2020): 500–522.

5. Adam L. Alter and Hal E. Hershfield, "People Search for Meaning When They Approach a New Decade in Chronological Age," *Proceedings of the National Academy of Sciences* 111, no. 48 (2014): 17066–17070.

6. R. Bhargave and T. Miron-Shatz, *Forty and Fabulous? Milestone Agers Assess Life Satisfaction More on Income Than Positive Emotions*, Working paper, University of Texas at San Antonio, San Antonio, 2012.

7. Robert Levine, *A Geography of Time: The Temporal Misadventures of a Social Psychologist* (New York: Basic, 1997).

8. Joel Waldfogel, "The Deadweight Loss of Christmas," *American Economic Review* 83, no. 5 (1993): 1328–1336.

9.   Jet G. Sanders and Rob Jenkins, "Weekly Fluctuations in Risk Tolerance and Voting Behaviour," *PLOS ONE* 11, no. 7 (2016): e0159017.

10.   Alice Gaby, "The Thaayorre Think of Time Like They Talk of Space," *Frontiers in Psychology* 3 (2012): 300.

11.   Paul Halsall, "Salimbene: On Frederick II, 13th Century," *Internet Medieval Sourcebook*, January 1, 1996, https://sourcebooks.fordham.edu/source /salimbene1.asp#:~:text=But%20he%20laboured%20in%20vain,of %20countenance%2C%20and%20blandishments.%20%22.

12.   M. Keith Chen, "The Effect of Language on Economic Behavior: Evidence from Savings Rates, Health Behaviors, and Retirement Assets," *American Economic Review* 103, no. 2 (2013): 690–731.

13.   Seán G. Roberts, James Winters, and Keith Chen, "Future Tense and Economic Decisions: Controlling for Cultural Evolution," *PLOS ONE* 10, no. 7 (2015): e0132145.

CHAPTER 16

1.   ABC News, "Defense Delivers Opening Statement in Derek Chauvin Trial," YouTube video, March 29, 2021, https://youtu.be/1RfRTnqL5bI.

2.   "Active/Passive Voice," CUNY School of Law, accessed January 2, 2023, https://www.law.cuny.edu/legal-writing/students/grammar/active-passive -voice.

3.   Philip N. Johnson-Laird, "Shorter Articles and Notes the Interpretation of the Passive Voice," *Quarterly Journal of Experimental Psychology* 20, no. 1 (1968): 69–73.

4.   Gerd Bohner, "Writing about Rape: Use of the Passive Voice and Other Distancing Text Features as an Expression of Perceived Responsibility of the Victim," *British Journal of Social Psychology* 40, no. 4 (2001): 515–529.

5.   Alexandra K. Frazer and Michelle D. Miller, "Double Standards in Sentence Structure: Passive Voice in Narratives Describing Domestic Violence," *Journal of Language and Social Psychology* 28, no. 1 (2009): 62–71.

6.   Ethan Kross, Emma Bruehlman-Senecal, Jiyoung Park, Aleah Burson, Adrienne Dougherty, Holly Shablack, Ryan Bremner, Jason Moser, and Ozlem

Ayduk, "Self-Talk as a Regulatory Mechanism: How You Do It Matters," *Journal of Personality and Social Psychology* 106, no. 2 (2014): 304.

7. Ethan Kross, Brian D. Vickers, Ariana Orvell, Izzy Gainsburg, Tim P. Moran, Margaret Boyer, John Jonides, Jason Moser, and Ozlem Ayduk, "Third-Person Self-Talk Reduces Ebola Worry and Risk Perception by Enhancing Rational Thinking," *Applied Psychology: Health and Well-Being* 9, no. 3 (2017): 387–409.

8. Robin Conley, "Living with the Decision That Someone Will Die: Linguistic Distance and Empathy in Jurors' Death Penalty Decisions," *Language in Society* 42, no. 5 (2013): 503–526.

9. Stephen Porter, Leanne ten Brinke, and Kevin Wilson, "Crime Profiles and Conditional Release Performance of Psychopathic and Non-Psychopathic Sexual Offenders," *Legal and Criminological Psychology* 14, no. 1 (2009): 109–118.

10. Jeffrey T. Hancock, Michael T. Woodworth, and Stephen Porter, "Hungry Like the Wolf: A Word-Pattern Analysis of the Language of Psychopaths," *Legal and Criminological Psychology* 18, no. 1 (2013): 102–114.

CHAPTER 17

1. Richard Orange, "Sweden Invents a Word for Girls' Genitals Equivalent to 'Willy' for Boys," *The Guardian*, August 1, 2015, https://www.theguardian.com/world/2015/aug/01/sweden-girls-genitals-feminist-invention-snippa-vagina.

2. Susan Sontag, *Illness as Metaphor* (New York: Farrar, Straus, and Giroux, 1977).

3. Hongchun Wang, Fang Zhao, Xiangling Wang, and Xiaoyang Chen, "To Tell or Not: The Chinese Doctors' Dilemma on Disclosure of a Cancer Diagnosis to the Patient," *Iranian Journal of Public Health* 47, no. 11 (2018): 1773.

4. David J. Hauser and Norbert Schwarz, "The War on Prevention: Bellicose Cancer Metaphors Hurt (Some) Prevention Intentions," *Personality and Social Psychology Bulletin* 41, no. 1 (2015): 66–77.

5. Paul H. Thibodeau and Lera Boroditsky, "Metaphors We Think With: The Role of Metaphor in Reasoning," *PLOS ONE* 6, no. 2 (2011): e16782.

6. "David Cameron: 'Swarm' of Migrants Crossing Mediterranean," *BBC News*, July 30, 2015, https://www.bbc.co.uk/news/av/uk-politics-33714282.

7. "Caricatures from Der StüRmer: 1933–1945," Calvin University German Propaganda Archives, January 1, 1998, https://research.calvin.edu/german-propaganda-archive/sturmer.htm.

8. Shantal R. Marshall and Jenessa R. Shapiro, "When 'Scurry' vs. 'Hurry' Makes the Difference: Vermin Metaphors, Disgust, and Anti-Immigrant Attitudes," *Journal of Social Issues* 74, no. 4 (2018): 774–789.

9. Mona El-Hout and Kristen Salomon, "Villains or Vermin? The Differential Effects of Criminal and Animal Rhetoric on Immigrant Cardiovascular Responses," *Group Processes & Intergroup Relations* 25, no. 8 (2022): 1939–1957.

10. Seyoung Lee and Thomas Hugh Feeley, "The Identifiable Victim Effect: A Meta-Analytic Review," *Social Influence* 11, no. 3 (2016): 199–215.

CHAPTER 18

1. "Bob Monkhouse: The Million Joke Man," *Gold TV*, accessed December 16, 2022, https://gold.uktv.co.uk/bob-monkhouse-million-joke-man/article/bobs-best-jokes/.

2. Arthur Schopenhauer, *The World as Will and Idea*, trans. R. B. Haldane and J. Kemp (London: Keegan Paul, Trench, Trubner, 1907).

3. William Hazlitt and Arnold Glover, *The Collected Works of William Hazlitt*, ed. A. R. Waller and A. Glover (London: J. M. Dent & Co., 1902), 5.

4. Travis Proulx and Steven J. Heine, "Connections from Kafka: Exposure to Meaning Threats Improves Implicit Learning of an Artificial Grammar," *Psychological Science* 20, no. 9 (2009): 1125–1131.

5. Herbert H. Haines, "Radical Flank Effects," in *The Wiley-Blackwell Encyclopedia of Social and Political Movements*, edited by David A. Snow, Donatella della Porta, Doug McAdam, and Bert Klandermans (Hoboken, NJ: Wiley, 2013).

6. Jennifer L. Doleac and Benjamin Hansen, "The Unintended Consequences of 'Ban the Box': Statistical Discrimination and Employment Outcomes When Criminal Histories Are Hidden," *Journal of Labor Economics* 38, no. 2 (2020): 321–374.

CONCLUSION

1. Franziska Funke, Linus Mattauch, Inge van den Bijgaart, H. Charles J. Godfray, Cameron Hepburn, David Klenert, Marco Springmann, and Nicolas Treich, "Toward Optimal Meat Pricing: Is It Time to Tax Meat Consumption?," *Review of Environmental Economics and Policy* 16, no. 2 (2022): 219–240.

2. See https://www.mackinac.org/about/authors/12.

3. Rachel Glennerster and Seema Jayachandran, "Think Globally, Act Globally: Opportunities to Mitigate Climate Change in Low- and Middle-Income Countries," forthcoming (2023).

Index